The Bear Slayer

The Bear Slayer

*

Women's Self Defense

Gerald W. Goble, Ph.D.

iUniverse, Inc.
New York Lincoln Shanghai

The Bear Slayer
Women's Self Defense

iUniverse books may be ordered through booksellers or by contacting:

iUniverse
2021 Pine Lake Road, Suite 100
Lincoln, NE 68512
www.iuniverse.com
1-800-Authors (1-800-288-4677)

Because of the dynamic nature of the Internet, any Web addresses or links contained in this book may have changed since publication and may no longer be valid.

The views expressed in this work are solely those of the author and do not necessarily reflect the views of the publisher, and the publisher hereby disclaims any responsibility for them.

This book describes the self defense techniques that are dangerous if done incorrectly or in the process of self defense. The reader does so at his own risk.

ISBN: 978-0-595-47879-8

Printed in the United States of America

This book is dedicated to the students of the MorRiDo Taekwondo School and to the women and girls that have taken self defense classes. The book is also dedicated to those girls and women that did not have the opportunity to attend classes and receive the resulting boost in self esteem, self confidence and empowerment that they brought.

Contents

List of Illustrations

Acknowledgments

I want to note the many people that helped in the validation of the material in this book, in particular Keely Dixon, Theresa Fraser, Claire Fraser, Victoria Alcazar, and Michelle King 1st Dan Black Belts; and Keith Dixon, and Reed Curl 2nd Dan Black Belt Instructors. Finally, a special appreciation is noted to the editor Ellen D. Morris.

1.

Be a Woman of The Village

If you are married or have a boy friend you know that when you need your companion he is never there. This is the way of companions. It is the way it has always been. Long ago the men leave the village to go hunting for meat for the village to eat leaving only the old people, children and women. In comes the bear. When the men come back with an empty sack and a long face from the hunt they ask, "What's for dinner?" The wife says, "Bear!" The men are never there when the car stops, the plumbing has trouble or the bear comes in. The women step up and do the job. If they had not stepped up then the men would have come back to the village to find no one and the species would have died out. Inside of every woman is a tiger or dragon that can be released.

The immediate problem with releasing the tiger inside is that women are generally nurturers. Nurturers are mostly responsible for caring for day to day for their family. This is why the image above of the women in the village taking on the bear is realistic. It is their job. This is the highest priority for the nurturer. It is primal. It is the lion taking care of her cub. It is the bird making a nest: soft, warm, and safe.

Women as nurturers tend to provide an environment that is harmonious for their family. A situation that requires self defense is not harmonious so there is a tendency to shrink away from doing what is necessary. The key is then for the nurturer to understand that if they want to return to a harmonious life they are going to have to deal with this aggressive person, deal with him quickly and with purpose so they can get back to harmony.

There is a tendency for nurturers to avoid confrontations and as a result there is a desire for harmony. Self defense is often about using a confrontation as a pivot point upon which you base your self defense routines. Confrontation now becomes a tool to use against the antagonist. This is one of the key principles of self defense, when a confrontation appears, relax, summon your inner energy and prepare for the defense.

The nurturer looks on herself as gentle and thoughtful. Nurturers have trouble making choices that could hurt others even if the one that is hurt is someone that is about to hurt them. The key here is to go back to the need to care for their family day to day. This is a higher priority need for the nurturer. If this attacker is between her and her need to care for her family from day to day then a defense against the attacker must be done. If you then couple this need with the knowledge of techniques that can be done that do not do permanent damage but allow her to escape the present situation then the nurturer has the power to defend herself and her family.

This book is for women, so the use of he, himself, him refer to the attacker, while the use of she, her, herself refers to defender. In writing this book we attempted to highlight how the natural instincts, behavior, movements, and body shape contribute to self defense. Every attempt is made to give the place and time where an attack can occur, as well as the possible motives and intent of the attacker. Understanding the environment of an attack provides the nurturer with a mental picture of what to avoid and using this knowledge to avoid an attack.

Women that have come to my school for self defense classes always ask *what if* questions about specific situations where they are concerned about. This is some situation they have heard that struck a cord in their mind a situation they do not want to be in. They read in the newspaper or hear on TV about the individual that was attacked by someone lurking under a car in a dark parking lot. Investigate the situation and read it in detail about it and consider if it makes sense to you. For example if you have a low car and not a high SUV he probably will not fit under the car. There are many good books on self defense but they are generally written for martial artists and not the novice.[1,2,3,4,5]

Part of learning self defense is to understand how and why it occurs. The first rule is *not looking at what you read in newspapers as representative* of what must be prepared for in self defense. News paper editors and reporters are trying to sell news papers so stories are valued on there attraction value. That is why you see the large headlines *The North Side Rapist Strikes Again.* A great deal is made of the stranger that comes in out of the dark to attack someone. This is not what the statistics say about who attacks who. Only a very small percentage of the women attacked are attacked by a stranger. The highest probability is that the attacker is someone the defender knows. The attacker most likely is a friend, relative, religious figure, lover, or husband. In the next section of the book you evaluate those about you and yourself. Use this section to find out whether you are making yourself a target by your actions or attitudes.

In teaching self defense over the years I have again and again been confronted with *the sending my little girl off to college syndrome.* This is where two months before their daughter goes to college in some other city the parents suddenly come to the realization that she needs some training on self defense. It would be better to bring her in three years earlier so she could have had healthy exercise, developed self confidence, and lots of practice in self defense. People have busy lives and not everyone can devote the time for training with the many other things in a young person's life, especially in high school. Having to deal with this problem many times I developed training methods to quickly address the highest priority items, give a few techniques for the most likely kind of attacks, and provide a useful document for them to read when they leave.

The layout of this book is set up to get to the most important concept and give background and philosophy later in the book. The descriptions are given almost totally in text. It is my experience that books with pictures or sketches often leave out much of the detail thinking. The picture will tell it all. If you are forced to write all of the details down then you need to write about every joint, every finger and the feelings you get in you finger tips, and your legs and feet.

The subject is daunting so only a few scenarios are chosen based on experience in teaching women's self defense as important and those illustrated with diagrams. The illustrations are crude and only give the spatial references of the individuals and sequences in the self defense routine. The first time reader using these few illustrated techniques can get useful information and begin the process of developing self confidence. After these important techniques there is a detailed listing of many other techniques broken down by area and kind of attack. Again, these techniques are chosen based on experience in teaching self defense in class as useful, simple, and effective.

Finally, this book is for the student that came in that was attacked. This book is for the student that could not stand to have someone closer than arms length. This book is for the student that cowers when an arm is raised or there is a large noise. And finally, this book is for the student that does not know what is about to happen to her. In leading some of these students back to self confidence it took a long time with incremental improvements, but they achieved it. So if you were attacked, abused or are afraid, then seek out a good martial arts school and kick, punch, and throw your way to self confidence. Choose the martial arts school using these simple rules, are there a lot of women that go to the school (women do not go where the environment is not good). Choose a place that is convenient (you will need to go often). And finally, choose a school that does not tie you up in a long contract process (you are not after a black belt but simple self defense).

2.

Questions the Village Shaman Will Ask

In every village there is an older woman that with her experience gives sage advice to the younger women. In this section the reader is asked some basic question about her intent and concepts. This is the basic Socratic method of teaching. Asking questions of the reader so in answering them becomes enlightened and understands what she really knew all along. So picture yourself in the village with the old woman that is the Shaman questioning your purpose.

Why are you here?

This is a basic requirement for women in self defense. Why do you want to learn self defense? You need to understand the basic questions here. Who do you fear? Do you have a history of abuse? Are you in a relationship with an abusive person? Must you work or travel in a dangerous environment? Are you here supporting someone else? Are you just here for the experience?

How urgent is your need to know self defense?

If you need to know self defense today at this minute to defend yourself then put down the book and go seek someone to help you. This book and the process of learning what is given here will take too long. It will take you time to grow in mind, spirit, and physical capabilities. If you have six months this book can help, but it will take time.

Are you ready to take care of yourself?

Your state of mind will determine how well you are able to perform self defense. You must have the state of mind that says, *I am going to do this, learn this and never live in fear again.* This is the state of mind that is your goal.

Are you trapped?

If you are trapped in an abusive relationship then this mental place is a distant place that may seem unattainable. Now you know that there is a bear fighter inside of you and you must let it grow. But with all things, in order for you to grow self confidence you need the proper environment. Like a flower in a garden needs to be free of weeds you may need to seek out a shelter so you can heal and grow. If you are trapped then it is time to break free and not look back. This situation is where the village women cluster about one of their own to protect her.

Are you ready to look at the world?

All men and women are basically the same. There is no perfect good in them. There is no evil in them. There is only humanness. From regressive DNA it appears presently that we all came from the same woman. This means we are all brothers and sisters, and we are all capable of doing great things since some of our brothers and sisters did so. However, we are capable of doing the worst of the bad things since some of our brothers and sisters did so. It means you can trust everyone and no one. To put it another way you know what everyone is capable of doing. You can look upon it as living with a tiger. As you walk with the tiger in the brush his movements are sleek and beautiful. You know he likes to snuggle next to you and have his ear scratched, but you know when he turns and looks at you in a certain way, you are on the menu. Something you just did made him think *prey for eating*. Part of self defense is living in the world with other humans and not indicating that you are prey.

Are you ready to critically look at yourself?

Women are nurturers. This is the quality that defines women. A woman understanding and practicing self defense will not affect her being a nurturer. The image of the Bear Slayer is slaying the bear while having a baby on one hip. To answer the question of this section may change the way you live, where you live, how you behave, how you dress, how you sense the world around you, and finally how you feel about yourself. During this book, many examples are presented of women's activities and behaviors which are problematic in the area of self defense. If you see one of these behavior characteristics in yourself then make note of it.

3.

Lessons from the Village Shaman

If you are the Bear Slayer then you need to look at the village around you. Since we are all part of the same family, we need to spend some time going over the world in which you live. We need to review how members of this village of man behave and how you can use what you know to defend yourself. It used to be true that when young women reached a certain age the older women in the village clustered around them to impart to them what they were going to need as adult women. Now such education appears to be spotty and incomplete.

Bad Behavior in Smaller Persons

In this chapter we look at how you behave in the world. You can stand in the willows and look out on the world and never be noticed. Under this camouflage you never have to face a predator. However, it is hard to live your life in the willows.

Doe Behavior

The doe look is that *what is going on here* look at the bright lights just before the truck turns her into a highway pizza. Here you see the violence about to happen to you and you stand there saying to yourself, *this can't be happening*. If you understand the predator/prey relationship you know inside you just haven't accepted that you are prey. A doe often ends up butchered.

Blind Obedience

Some cultures demand blind obedience to their husband by the wife. A symptom of this is the opinion that *right or wrong the man has the final say*. Who came up with something so stupid some man? No one is perfect therefore relying on someone to have the final say means double stupidity. First the stupidity of the man in some decision he makes that is wrong and the stupidity of you for following a stupid decision. The trouble with obedience is that if you disobey, then to get you back into the obedience mode you must be punished. When you first train a dog you use a choke chain and hard jerks along with a firm *No* followed by a sweet sounding *Good Boy*. If you relax your training, the dog will revert to its old ways. In the abusive situation there is the abuse followed by an apology, but like the dog the female has already been pulled back in line so the sweet sounds are only to keep you in line. A physical attribute someone else sees of this behavior in the woman or child that is in this situation is the quick look downward when a hand is raised or a voice is raised.

Allowing Fawning Behavior

Teen age girls do this with their boyfriends. You see it in public with two teenagers walking with their arms around each other as they walk. A hug is a hug, but a hug that goes on as you are walking is fawning. The question that needs to be asked is *Who are you, his mama?* This is bad training on both the girl's and boyfriend's part. The girl is now set up for a future confrontation when she does not want to do the behavior. The boy is now setup for a future confrontation with some other female that does not want such behavior. In the animal world this is called grooming, however teenage girls rarely get rid of any fleas. The problem is that teenage boys are particularly shallow and will assume that their next girlfriend is required to fawn all over them, and this sets up the next girl for a confrontation. Unless corrected, this will lead to an individual that needs to control every aspect of your behavior which is one step away from a chronic abuser.

I Can Change Him

This represents another shallow understanding of mankind on behalf of the female that says such a stupid thing. Change comes from the inside. It never comes from the outside. Even for those young men that think they have been changed by Basic Training in the military, the drill instructor did not change them. These young men changed because they realized the sense of it. Further, change must be proven with period of changed behavior. If you have known Mr. A for three years and he was a jerk for 3 years then proof he is not a jerk takes three years. The female that thinks she can change someone is setting herself up for a problem.

Undisciplined Intake of Chemicals

Excessive drinking, binge drinking or drugs is not good. The use of alcohol requires discipline. It is easy to use it at the wrong time and in too much quantity. It makes you feel good. It lowers your defenses. Lowering your defenses is not what self defense is about.

Passing off fault and responsibility

An adult accepts responsibility for her actions. An adult expects other adults to except responsibility for their actions. If you pass off blame for something you have done to someone else you need to grow-up. If you pass off blame for something your mate or boy friend has done to someone else, you need to grow up. If you or your boyfriend were tricked into doing something bad or stupid then stand up and smarten up.

Bad Mouth, Bad Dress, Bad Manners

Just like the example of walking with a tiger, behaving like prey gets you preyed upon. Good, bad, right, or wrong, people treat you like what you look like. This may be a bad thing but it helps people in society sort out the rest of the community into people they can trust and people they cannot trust. This is communal self defense. Society defines certain behavior as bad because they know it attracts predators. Therefore for their own protection they shun certain behavior. Examples of this kind of behavior are as follows: inappropriate dress such as skirts too short, too much exposed midriff, too much or too strange make-up or hair styles, etc.; inappropriate behavior such as flashing, wet tee shirt contests, lurid dancing etc; inappropriate language such as using of too many swear words.

History of Abuse

Abused individuals abuse others or ignore abuse in others. If you were abused in the past and have not sought help then seek it.

Bad Behavior in Larger Person

Undisciplined intake of chemicals

Excessive drinking, binge drinking or drugs is not good. The use of alcohol requires discipline. It is easy to use it at the wrong time and in too much quantity. It makes you feel good. It lowers your inhibitions. If you have a predilection for violence then excessive use of chemicals makes it easier. To go back to the example of the tiger, excessive chemical intake is like taking off the collar and chain. This is a person to avoid.

Argumentative Behavior

Individuals that drop into argumentative behavior with the slightest provocation have internal difficulties that must be resolved. Dropping into argumentative behavior is a release from these problems. Release makes the person feel better but the level of the behavior accelerates. Unless the underlying cause is dealt with and quickly then violence will follow. You have seen this person. He will raise his voice in a public area then turn to someone he does not know and ask in a loud voice, *What are you looking at?* This is a person to avoid.

Controlling Behavior

The individual that feels he needs to control your every aspect is insecure about your relationship. If he must control how you look; who you see; where you go; what you do; and control your finances to the dime then he is very insecure. If you try to do something on your own or something of which he does not approve then you must be jerked back in line somehow. This is one step away from abuse. This is a person to avoid.

Passing off fault and responsibility

An adult accepts responsibility for his actions. An adult expects other adults to except responsibility for their actions. If he passes off blame for something he has done to someone else he needs to grow-up. If he was tricked into doing something bad or stupid then he should stand up and smarten up. This is a person to avoid.

Bad mouth bad dress, bad manners

Just like the example of someone walking with a tiger, if you are dealing with someone that looks like a tiger, smells like a tiger, behaves like a tiger then your acting like prey is not good. Good, bad, right, or wrong, people treat you like what you look like. They do this because of experience. This may be a bad thing but it helps people in society sort out the rest of the community into people they can trust and people they cannot trust. This is communal self defense. Society defines certain behavior as bad because they know it defines predators. Therefore for their own protection they shun certain behavior. Examples of this kind of behavior are as follows: inappropriate dress such as obscene tee shirts; strange hair styles, etc.; inappropriate behavior; inappropriate language such as using of too many swear words. This is a person to avoid.

History of Abuse

Abused individuals abuse others or ignore abuse in others. If you are dealing with a male that was abused in the past and has not sought help then he must seek it. If this is not done then he is an abuse time bomb waiting to go off.

Play Bill—Telling Bad Guys from Good Guys

After the discussion about bad behavior the question arises, *How do you tell the good guys from the bad guys*? Going back to the indication from DNA that we are all of the same family, then we are all similar and you need to rely on social criteria for distinguishing.

The best approach is to have some idea how the individual you are dealing with makes his decisions. If he were to list in priority what is important then you know what he puts first. We all know people we consider in the good guy these individuals have a priority system. If we look at what society considers a good guy for example we can look at movies with the quintessential or cowboy or frontiersman. They have a code, *The Code of the West*. This code is based on protecting your loved ones riding across the plains in a covered wagon. It is *seeing to your family, your live stock, your leathers and then yourself*. Based on this code, given below are two lists one for an adult male and one for a young male.

Adult Male
1) Wife and Children,
2) Parents,
3) Job, stuff needed for 1&2,

4)   Others ordered by how helpless they are (Old People, Animals, Friends, etc.)

5)   Himself and his fun things.

Young Male

1)   Parents

2)   School Work & stuff needed for 1,

3)   Others ordered by how helpless they are (Old People, Animals, etc.)

4)   Girl Friend and other friends

5)   Himself and his fun things.

Let us now look at what this list reveals. First, the good guy puts his own requirements last in both lists. The lists are generally ordered with those he is committed to and the helpless he puts before others, he enjoys and always before himself. If you have an individual that puts himself and his things before family or the helpless then he will always do the wrong thing which will land him in difficulty and open you if you are close to him to his lashing out. When he lashes out he will make excuses and blame others for the situation he has gotten himself into.

Behavior Signs

When you walk with a tiger and the tiger ignores or approves of your presence then you know it. Your primal senses will tell you that you are OK. If you walk with a tiger and you get that certain look that indicates to you are potentially on the menu, you will also know this because of your primal senses. That is a behavior sign of the tiger. Now most of us do not walk with tigers, but we do know people that we do not trust. Often it is just a feeling which discount.

If we are talking, working or otherwise interacting with someone then we can get certain reactions from our interactions. In some cases these interactions indicate the relationship is potentially hostile. Often these are the result of hand gestures, body positions or movements, eye movements, sweat, color or other physical indication. These are the behavior signs of another kind of predator. Most of us know what these indications are but below we will list a few of them.

Anger

In anger sometimes you see an individual that is red faced, or with expanded veins in his forehead, with gritted teeth, shaking hands or squinted eyes. All of these are indications that individual is holding in anger. Your mother knew all of these signs and if you were a child prone to anger it got you a time out or other punishment. The predator does not have a mother to give him a time out before he commits the assault.

So what to do? Whatever it is, you must be casual. This is time for you to do the "earring fiddle". The earring fiddle is a casual way to assume a defensive position, see the appendix on terminology. Take a position which is beyond the ability of the antagonist to make a quick strike at you. This is called the first strike position. Be casual in your behavior.

In this angry state the antagonist can walk away and shed his anger through some physical tantrum or some verbal rant. He can however, just as easily attack to vent the anger. The trigger can be almost anything so there is no set response. Trying to make light of the situation can just as easily set him off as defuse the situation. Trying to make a logical argument, changing the subject, sympathizing with him, or many other approaches can also either defuse or set off the situation. There is no magic bullet at this juncture, but if you study people and their behavior you will have better luck in choosing the correct path. You do know one thing. You have to put your self at a distance to where you have a 1 to 2 second lead time in any attack because he must now step toward you.

Fear

Fear is characterized by other face signs such as a loss of color, looking down and shuffling the feet, biting the lower lip, diverting the eyes or looking from side to side, and ducking the head. Your mother also knew all of these signs and when she saw them the result was a deeper inquiry into what you were up to. You can bet that the average predator knows them also and will take advantage of them.

This is another place for the earring fiddle only here instead of fiddling with your earring rub the side of your face. The friction of rubbing will cause a slight highlight in your cheek. This highlight is enough to reduce the outward sign of fear by a loss of color in the face, while keeping your hands in the correct position. Further by just placing yourself in the yin yang position with your hands you will have less fear. The samurai Tsunetomo in the Hagakure[7] tells of a procedure where you lick your finger and run it around the upper part of the inside of your ear to increase your alertness. In each of these cases you do something physical that is used as a physiological crutch or buttress to allow you to overcome the fear. You should also place yourself at a distance of more than an arm's length but you cannot show signs of moving backward because that generally will cause the antagonist to do more of what caused the fear reaction.

Good and bad response

To diffuse a situation where you are confronting someone the response can be a variety of things: anger and fear, soothing voice and sarcasm, insult and nervousness, humor and boredom. In any situation the response you choose can be wrong or right. You will never know because you have no idea of his lifetime of interactions with others. Your soothing voice might remind him of some antagonist 20 years ago and set him off, or it might remind him of someone that soothed his injured spirit.

Whatever you try in an effort to talk your way out of the situation is a good response. If you can talk your way out of the situation then that is a good thing. But you cannot trust yourself to talk your way out of every confrontation. The reason it is a good response is that it gives you time to assess the physical situation for escape routes, places to strike on the antagonist if you must, and the opportunity to casually move to a better location incase of a you are faced with conflict. As you are talking you shift your stance to a lower stance, a stance that allows you to go directly into a vigorous self defense. (The most complete description of this stance is given by Miyamoto Musashi. [8, 9], see the appendix on terminology). In doing this you have taken on the roll of the predator, stalking your opponent.

Boundaries

There are boundaries between individuals and they are the limits of respect. When you define respect there are several areas defined as limits. Respect is treating someone well, treating someone's stuff well, treating someone's space well, and treating someone's feelings well.

Touching is one of these boundaries. It is the physical representation of respect. Whether touching is respectful or not is determined by the norms of the society to which you belong and is dependent on who is doing the touching and who is receiving the touch as to weather it is respectful.

The person that is doing the touch can be defined as mother, father, friend same sex, friend other sex, acquaintance, and stranger. The where of the touch is also important: head, hands, and feet, back of upper body, legs, front of the upper body, back of the hip area, and front of the hip area. If we ask individuals how they feel about the various touching by various people then we can develop a complete picture of the norms of the society in which you live. But most of us know what is proper and improper in touching activities. Touching also is the legal boundary for assault.

When you do not treat someone's stuff or their space well you risk a suit. The boundaries for civil law suit are well known. If something bad happens then sue everyone within eyesight. This is another boundary of respect.

When you do not treat someone's feelings well again there are limits. The upper limit is verbal assault. If you get in someone's face and yell and scream enough to put them in fear for their life then you are guilty of verbal assault. This is part of the classic abuse of the spouse to follow up the physical abuse with verbal abuse to the point where the one receiving the assault becomes submissive.

Lessons Learned

In understanding anything you always look back to history or others that were the target of attacks or required to use self defense. What are the lessons learned from such an event?

Here are some common answers for the attacked individual.

It wasn't your fault. The answer may or not be true. Remember the deer looking out from the brush into the open plain. He smells a faint sense of lion but does not see one and ventures out only to find himself as dinner. In self defense the situation is similar. You may have done something to attract the predator. You may have ignored your senses that were trying to tell you the situation in front of you was dangerous. The teenage girl with the face that shows her insecurity, a timid demeanor, and dressed to try to fit in is prime meat for the predator. So it wasn't your fault but if you act like the deer you attract hunters.

You have the right to go where you want and do what you want. Again this may or may not be true. If you are in a theater you do not have the right to yell fire for no reason. You have a right to climb into a cage with a lion, but your right may injure someone getting into the cage to drag your lifeless body out. Should the lion be killed for your stupidity? Clearly the statement is not true. If you tease a dog when it is young it will grow into a dog that has an unpleasant disposition. If you go someplace you should not and are in court to accuse someone that has attacked you then it is considered in the defense of the attacker by the jury. Clearly do not go where you should not. This requires you to have some sense about you and to know what environment you are about to enter.

You didn't do anything wrong. That depends on the definition of wrong. If wrong includes behavior that attracts predators it is clearly not true. Some of us by our very nature attract predators. To avoid attracting a predator when this attractive behavior is part of your nature is a hard thing to do. Therefore if you are one of those that attract predators then you must be very careful about what you do.

Rape is an assault. If rape is an assault then you need to treat it as such. This leads to self defense of the highest order. There is no reason to ever hold back in your counter attack.

Is there something I could have done to avoid it? Is there something I could have done to fight back? If I had only ... Not been there ... Not allowed him to control me ... Known what to do. Now you are asking the right questions. Now you can begin the training you need.

Dressing For the Event!

Can you run away? If you have glumpy shoes that will not allow you to run then expect to shed them and run bare foot. If your skirt will not allow you to run the shed the modesty, pick up your skirt and run.

Can you kick waist high? If you cannot kick waist high then groin kicks are out. Again be prepared to hike up your skirt if you need to, modesty is a luxury.

Can your clothing be used against you? Can your clothing be grabbed to pull you down to the ground? Items such as long scarves, capes and items that drape can be problematic.

This is not to say you cannot wear stylish cloths or you need to dress like a solider. But if you are going home from the opera, you are in the garage with your flowing gown, long scarf, and 3 inch heels then are prepared to shed the fancies turn and face your attacker. If you subdue your attacker sufficiently then put on your shoes, pick up your scarf and leave.

4.

Today's Bear

This section of the book is to give a quick and dirty set of techniques that are useful, easily learned, and appear often in self defense situations. Given here are a few important techniques for common situations that have appeared in particular to women. The sketches are given only for the reader to have spatial sense of the action. Considerable research on common attacks has established these scenarios.

The procedure used is the same for all of the scenarios. Once the attack has begun, the defender shocks the attacker, escapes any holds, counters with multiple strikes until the attacker is sufficiently distracted and then runs for safety. The multiple strike routines generally are done in a high low fashion striking any target on the attacker that is available and where pain can be delivered to the attacker. The high low approach is to strike the face, throat, eyes and other high points and feet, shins, knees and groin and other low points in an alternate manner. This approach gives a specific set of possibilities for blocking strikes or hiding targets that choosing a specific set of targets in a specific sequence would invariably end in a sequence that would not work.

Bully Push

The attack is a bully push. This is a shove with both hands on the upper body. This type of attack usually occurs in close situations such at a crowded area and often occurs in low places such as bars, dance halls etc. The first recommendation is don't go to such places. Now such an attack rarely comes from a man to a woman but more often between people of the same sex. The attack does not come all at once but is the end point of a verbal confrontation.

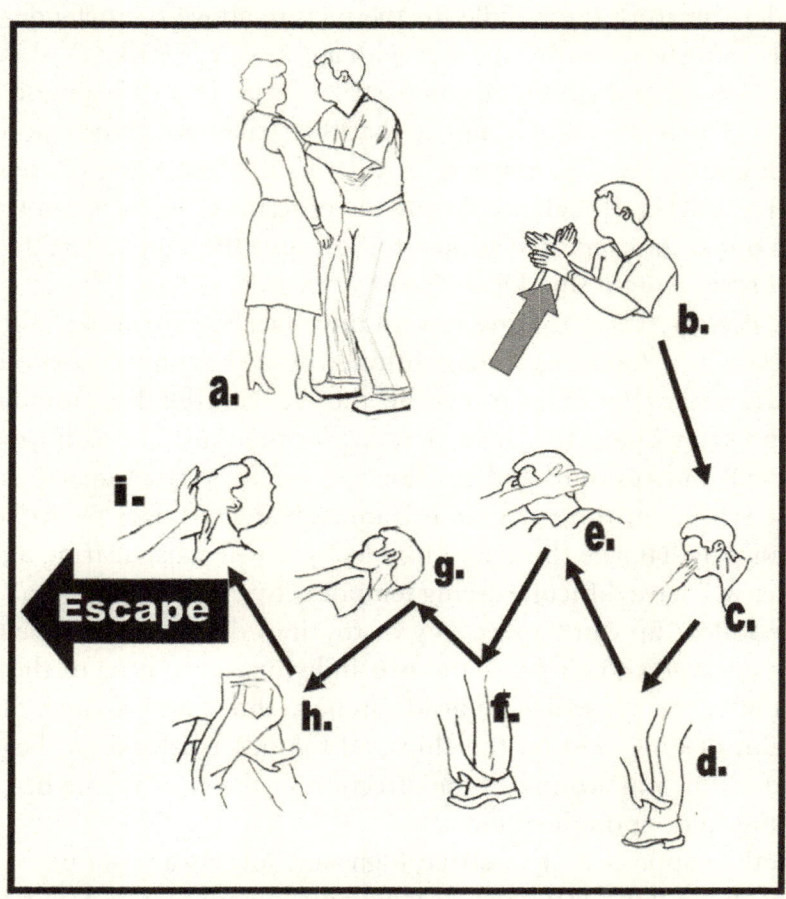

Figure 1: Bully Push

As the situation develops the defender should assume a lower stance with the knees slightly bent and if possible turned slightly away. The defense shown here is called a *preying hand* defense. As the attack occurs the defender is shoved backward. The defender slides the one foot back to assume a wider and lower stance. The defender will feel the calf of the leg that is slid backward tighten. Since the bully will pursue in the attack there is a second push. If the push has two hands the defender's hands are brought up into a *preying hand position*. The hands are brought up between the pushing hands to spread them apart as in b) above, so the defender can *work* the middle. In the picture above the defender goes directly into shocking the attacker with a double eye strike c), shin kick d), ear slap e), foot stomp f), elbow strike g), groin strike h), and palm strike i). The reader should notice that the strikes go from high to low to high and so on. The key here is to strike the first thing in view and keep the attacker off balance during the procedure. These are not single strikes but each is repeated strikes, for example the shin kick really consists of several rapid shin kicks (3 or 4 work well).

The defenders hands move toward the attackers face and eyes fingertips first. The defender screams continuously as the counter goes on. The defender strikes the cheek just below the eye with the three middle fingers and she will feel the cheek bone under the skin. The skin from the cheek will slide upward and cushion the eye from the finger tips during the strike. For the nurturer, it is unlikely that a finger tip strike will permanently damage the eyes. More likely it will cause tearing and the attacker will have difficulty seeing temporarily.

The follow-up can be a variety of routines depending on the availability of targets to strike. If the two individuals are near to the same height after the eye strike the head can be grabbed and twisted. Placing the palm of one hand on the chin and the other behind the head the defender can spin around in the direction of the twist of the head and place the attacker on the floor.

Another approach is to strike high and low in alternating succession. Kick the shins. Slap the ears with cupped hands. Stomp on the feet. Palm strike the face. Knee the groin. All of these strikes must be done in quick succession. At this point with either of the approaches above, if the strikes were done well the defender should be able to escape. This is the desired end point of the defense. For additional information on these strikes see the appendix on terminology.

Face Slap or Back of the Hand

This is a frequent attack for the abused wife. It is used to bring the female back into a behavior mode consistent with the needs of the male. Again this does not come without signals: a motion, a look, a sound, an argument or some other signal. As in the above self defense routine the hands should be put in what is called the yin yang position with one high and one low. The upper hand can casually fondle with the earring while the lower hand fiddles with a button on the blouse. For this reason it is called the Earring Fiddle for a short name. It is a casual position that the defender can assume with out looking defensive. It is much like a boxer's stance but completely unassuming and even pensive looking. Watch the action without fixating on one thing or another and the defender should push slightly up on the toes to get the feeling of lightness in the heels of the feet.

As the attack comes there are a couple of approaches. The defender can work on the inside of the strike, that is, with the striking arm outside of the defender. The defender can also work on the outside of the strike, that is, with the striking arm pinned between the attacker and defender.

The first option is illustrated in the diagram. As the strike comes the upper hand deflects it along enough to bring up the lower hand to take its place. The upper hand should not try to stop the strike and the defender should move backward using the upper arm to push off. The defender will feel the wrist of the attacker in her palm of the upper hand. The lower hand comes straight upward and presses the back of the hand against the attackers inside wrist. The timing is such that the attacker is drawing back the hand and is easily pushed outward. The upper hand then draws backward and downward and strikes with a palm strike to the face. The heel of the palm strikes the front of the sliding up to the nose.

The defender will feel the skin of the chin slide under the strike and the nose pull upward. The nurturer should not be afraid of this strike. The lips will rub against the teeth and may cut the lip and cause bleeding but in a week it will heal. The nose may bleed but a little ice and this will heal quickly. Both are a small price to pay for a bad guy picking on a woman.

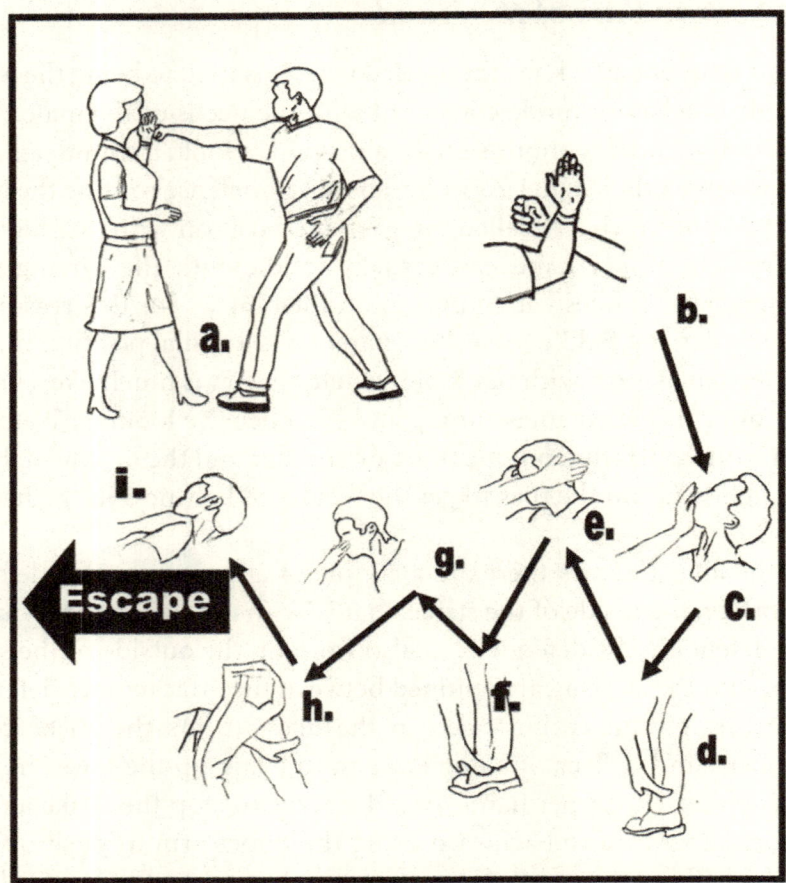

Figure 2: Slap or Punch to Face

Following this initial strike to cause tearing in the eye the defender should use multiple strikes alternating high and low in rapid succession. Kick the shins. Slap the ears with cupped hands. Stomp on the feet. Palm the face. Knee the groin. When the attacker is sufficiently distracted she can escape. The defender should notice the similar pattern with the bully push where the tactics of the counter is to strike multiple targets in an up down manner.

The pinning approach works in the following manner. As the attack comes the upper hand is used to deflect the strike while the face is drawn backward out of the way. The defender deflects the strike with a light touch at 90 degrees to the striking motion to a position where the striking arm can be pinned to the attacker's body. An example is as follows: for the attacker's right hand strike, the defender's left hand pushes on the outside of the striking arm downward so the attacker's arm is downward across the attacker's body. The defender brings her right hand up pinning the attacking arm to the attacker's body allowing the left hand to strike at the attacker at the face. After the strike the left hand can take the place of the right to continue pinning while the right hand is used for another strike.

After the strikes to the face the defender positions her body to the side. At this point she delivers a side kick to the side of the knee which should drop the attacker to one knee. Another kick that can be used if the angle is not right is a round house kick. A second side kick to the back will allow the defender to escape. The pinning of the striking hand and the two palm strikes and the side kick to the knee must be done very rapidly, *within one or two seconds*, while screaming

Clothing Grab Front High

This is the get into your face, violate your space, intimidate you attack. The grab is with one or both hands to the clothing at the neck level. There are many possible counters to this attack. For example a quick knee to the groin if he is using both hands for the grab. Another approach might be to just shed the garment, modesty is overrated anyway. Chopping arm at the elbow to create an elbow crank followed by an ax kick sweep is another possible technique.

A common escape, and the one illustrated below, is to use the insufficiencies of the hand. The hand is weak in the thumb and the little finger and either one can be peeled away to escape the hold. The technique given here uses a thumb fold which is particularly useful if the two individuals have approximately the same size hands.

The defender first strikes the face with a palm strike to shock the opponent. While the attacker is distracted by the shock of the palm strike the defender holds the attacker's wrist with one hand and squeezes the attacker's thumb with the other. The defender will feel the fingernail of the thumb pressing into the palm under the thumb. The pain delivered by squeezing the thumb closed will release the grab to the clothing. Following up with multiple strikes to all the targets the defender can see in rapid succession she should be able to escape.

Another approach is to use an Arm Bar. The arm bar will generally result in the attacker and defender at 90 degrees to each other with the defender facing the side of the attacker. Once the arm bar is formed the attacker will try to pull back so the legs must be kicked quickly to take the attacker down.

For the case where the attacker grabs with both hands and is nearly equal in height with the defender the first strike can be a kick to the groin, a double cupped hand strike to the ears, repeated kicks to the shins, double gouges to the eyes with the thumbs, and stomps to the instep of the feet. This should free you and have the attacker in tears which will allow you to escape. Notice the counters come in a high, low, high, low manner.

For the persons of lesser height a kick to the groin may be hard to accomplish. If the attacker lifts you off the ground for the attack it may position you for a knee to the groin. Otherwise gouge the eyes as the first strike. The nurturer should read the description of striking the eyes given above. Then the defender strikes the available targets as above until there is an opportunity for escape.

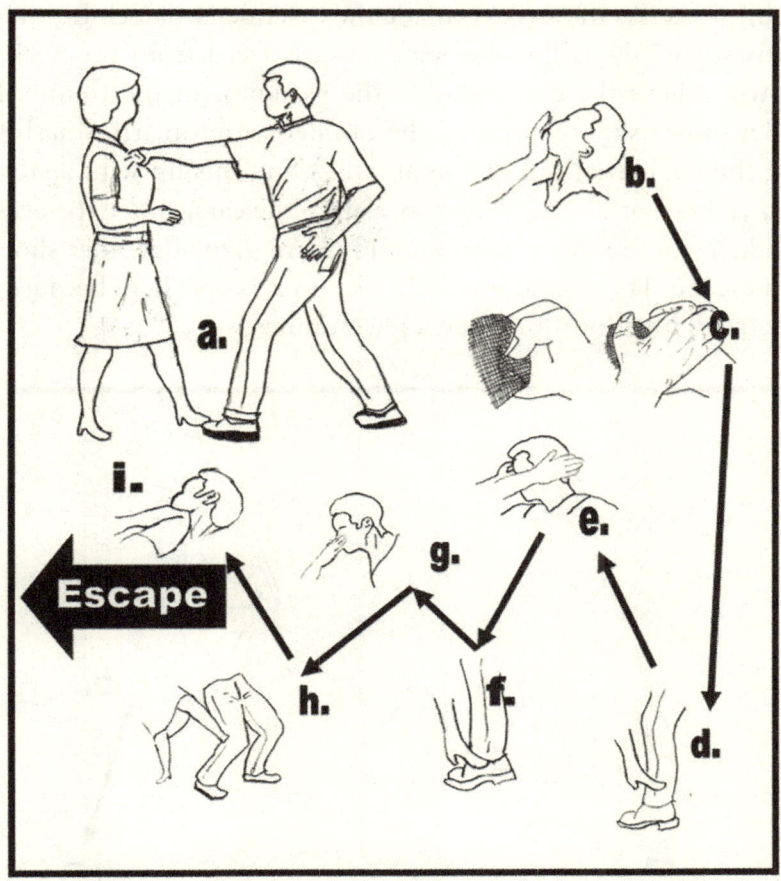

Figure 3: Grab to Clothing

Choke from Front Single Hand

In this choke the defender is pinned against a wall with a single hand to the throat. The defender cannot focus on the choke or she is in trouble. This is not a time for the nurturer to have any indecision, for she must act quickly. First the defender shocks the opponent with a kick to the shins, a palm strike to. the face, or both. This is followed by a palm strike across to the choking hand on the inside just above the thumb. The defender will feel the outward edge of the thumb with the heel of the palm strike. As the strike is made the defender will feel the attacker's hand twist slightly as the attacker's hand is freed from the neck. This strike will relieve the choke due to the weakness of the thumb. If the defender moves slightly forward she can deliver a forearm smash to the side of the attackers head or throat. Following this up with a stomp to the foot, a knee or kick to the groin, slap to the ears, gouge the eyes, and several kicks to the shins, all in a rapid manner, the defender should be able to escape. The nurturer should feel no remorse here because none of the strikes hurt for more than a few minutes

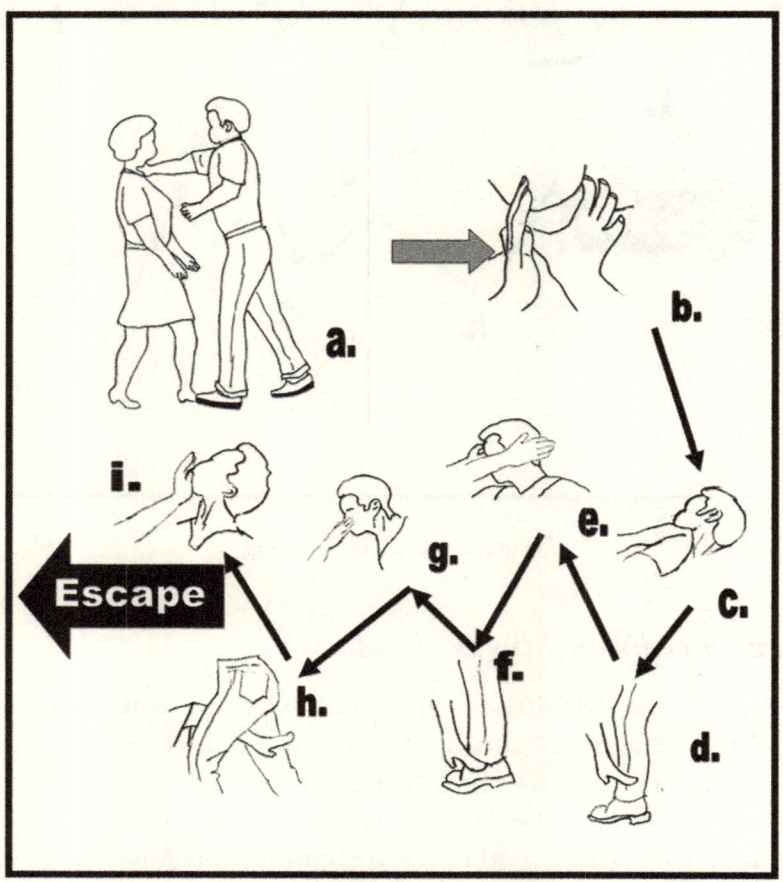

Figure 4: Single Hand Choke

An alternate method is to shock the attacker and then reach over the hand, grab the chopping edge of the hand and twist it backwards in the direction of the thumb. As the defender's hand does the grab she will feel in her finger tips pass over the hardness of the back and then the softness of the chopping edge. The thumbnail presses into the pressure point between the thumb and first finger. The defender will feel the softness of the area and the bone of the thumb, but to use the pressure point she needs to push as if to go under the thumb. If done correctly the hand will easily be removed from the grip. Once the arm bar is generated, it is followed by a foot stomp, strike to the eyes, and a kick to the back of the knees.

Hair Grab Front

It becomes very apparent in this attack that the defender should not resist. To do so causes immediate pain. To stop the pain of pulled hair press downward on top of the attacker's hand. Press it hard in place against the skull and press the head upward so the hand cannot move. The defender will feel the fist spread under the pressure. Then the defender twists her body in a direction that is toward the back of the attacker's wrist at the same time bending downward.

The result creates an arm bar and hand crank with the attackers grabbing hand. By pulling downward on the attacker's elbow and shoving the attackers hand toward the elbow the arm bar is complete. This is followed up with sufficient counters to allow escape of the defender.

An alternate routine is to hold the hand in place and run toward the attacker. The defender will generally be able to run faster and better forward than the attacker can run backward. The attacker will tend to fall backward and let go of the hair to use his hand to break his fall. This technique however requires space to complete and cannot be used in a confined area.

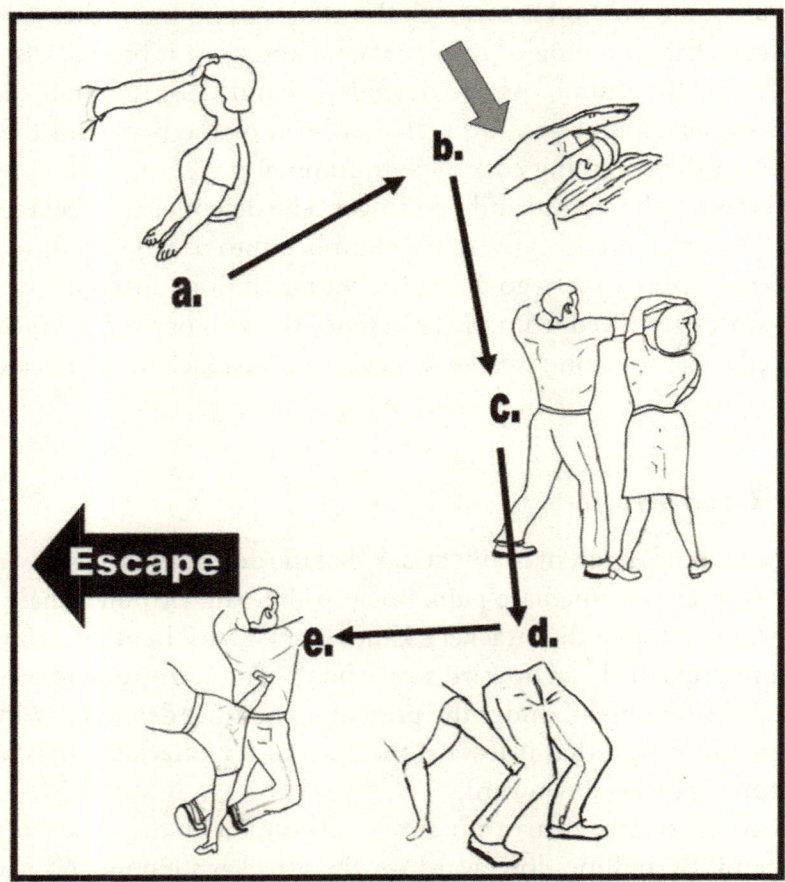

Figure 5: Hair Grab

Belly Strike

Women have an instinctual need to protect their face, breasts, and belly so any strike to these areas is meant to intimidate. An attack of this type will not happen instantly. There is a period before the strike where the attacker has a discussion with the defender. This is a build up period for the attacker and should be a key for the defender to take a defensive position.

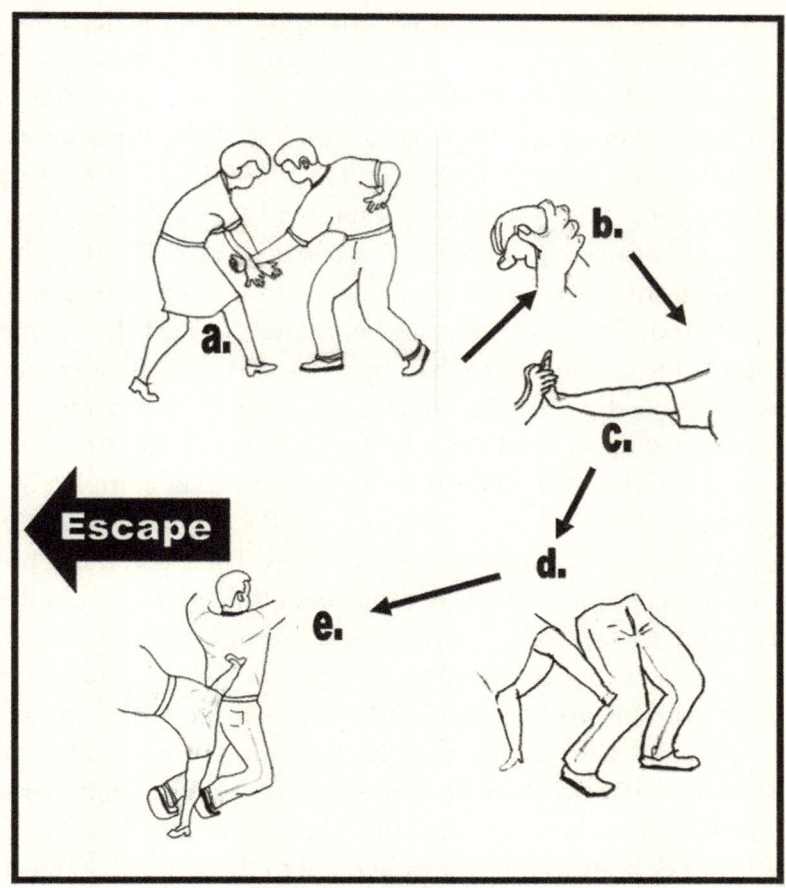

Figure 6: Belly Strike

The position at a minimum should be a non-apparent yin-yang hand position such as the ear ring fiddle but lower say fiddling with the upper button on the blouse and the belt buckle. There is no apparent particular signal that the defender should use the lower defensive position. The instinctual need will generally provide the feeling that the defender must be lower. Perhaps it is the attacker having his arms down that drives it but if the defender listens to her instincts she will know.

The attack comes in a low upward arc. The defender brings both wrists together in a butterfly hand configuration (also called an open hand X block). If the attacker is attacking with his right hand the defender must have her right hand on top in making the butterfly hands and reverse for the other attack. As the hands stop the forward and upward motion the defender slips her body back slightly to avoid the strike. Both hands close around the fist and wrist of the attacker. The top hand will close grabbing the chopping edge of the attacking hand; again the defender uses the senses in her fingertips to assure the grip is correct. The stopping and gripping of the attacking hand must be done in about a second or he will retract his hand. The attacker's hand is rotated toward the thumb and raised upward to create an arm bar. In doing this the defender will turn sideways and thereby force the attacker to turn in a like manner. This is quickly followed up by a side kick to the knee to take the attacker down to one knee. Another kick to the back will take attacker completely down allowing escape.

Would a nurturer do this? The answer is yes. There should be no, hesitation in the decision process because once the strike is initiated the defender knows two things 1) this person is a bad guy and all rules are off, and 2) there is soon a second strike if you do not act now.

This defense appears complex until it is practiced, but there are other options to explore. Let us say the defender wasn't paying attention or was just trying to ignore the jerk, then she is in a position with her hands down. As the strike comes forward the defender moves the hand on the same side of her body as the attacking hand to the outside of the attacking hand. The defenders hand should be in a praising hand position to allow her to push the attacking hand in the direction of the center of the attacker to deflect the strike away.

By committing himself to the lower strike almost always his face is open for a strike from the upper hand. The defender immediately strikes the philtrum of the mouth with a palm heel strike in an upward manner with full power. At this point the defender uses the up down striking method to strike alternately high and low targets on the attacker in a staccato like manner until an escape can be made. This approach requires faster reactions on the part of the defender.

Grab the wrist with one hand

The nurturer is assumed as more sensitive or to put it another way have higher senses. If someone attempts to grab the defender's wrist she should quickly pull it away and avoid the problem. But if for some reason the defender is grabbed at the wrist. There are several types of grabs: cross grabs, same arm grabs and two hand grabs. The common link is not to not pull back because that will make the attacker's grip tighten.

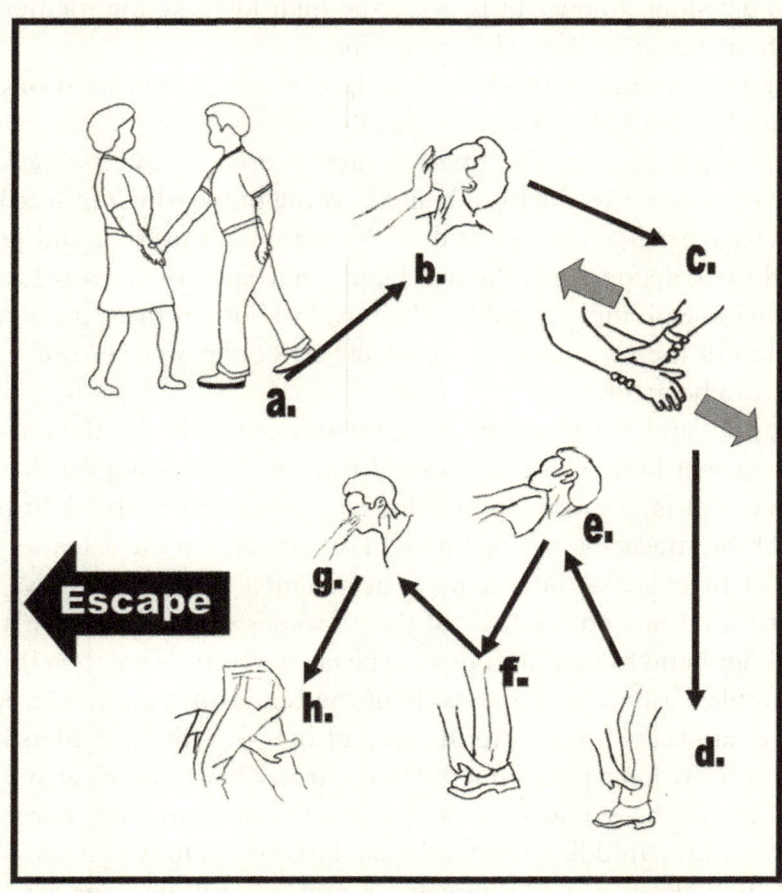

Figure 7: Grab to the Wrist

Make a *live hand* for the hand that is grabbed by opening the fingers all of the way. This will make the wrist stronger and the grip weaker. For a grab of a single arm of the defender, shock the opponent with the other hand or with a kick. The shock can be a palm strike or a shin kick. The palm strike is preferred since the attacker will have tears in his eyes. The defender grabs the captured hand with her other hand and pulls up sharply against the attacker's thumb. The use of two hands against one will easily free her from the grip.

The defender follows up is using the high low striking method in a staccato like manner until she can escape.

There are several methods in dealing with a captured wrist once the attacker is distracted with a sufficient shock.

Spear hand Escape: The finger escape is used by pulling backward on the little finger or the thumb and twisting outward with the gripped arm. The spear hand escape is done by grabbing the wrist and pulling toward the defender with the free hand while spearing forward toward the attacker with the gripped hand or arm. In both of these counters the next step in the routine is to repeatedly strike the attacker until a safe escape can be made.

Escaping and Pinning: These techniques generally use the attacker's elbow against him. There are several routines depending on the grab. The one that is discussed here is for an inside wrist grab (right or left hand of the attacker grabbing the right or left hand of the defender). The defender first shocks the attacker. The defender then makes a live hand and presses down on the back of the attacker's gripping hand with the heel of her hand to hold it in place. The gripped hands are then brought in a circular fashion to the outside of the center of the attacker. As the gripped hands are brought to the apex of the circle the defenders hands form butterfly hands gripping the lower arm. The attacker's arm is then locked about the elbow. By pulling rapidly downward and turning the arm toward the middle the attacker can be brought to the ground.

The best defense is not allowing a grab by pulling your arm away when the grab starts. In self defense classes this pulling back before you are grabbed is practiced thousands of times to increase reflexes.

Come Here Babe

This attack is where after some discussion the defender turns to leave. The attacker then reaches out to grasp the upper part of the arm and pull her back toward him, which is where this attack gets its name. The defense starts with non-resistance. Go with the pull rotating in to deliver a strike to the face, head or throat. If the defender and attacker are of equal height then a forearm smash is a good strike to deliver to the lower part of the face or throat.

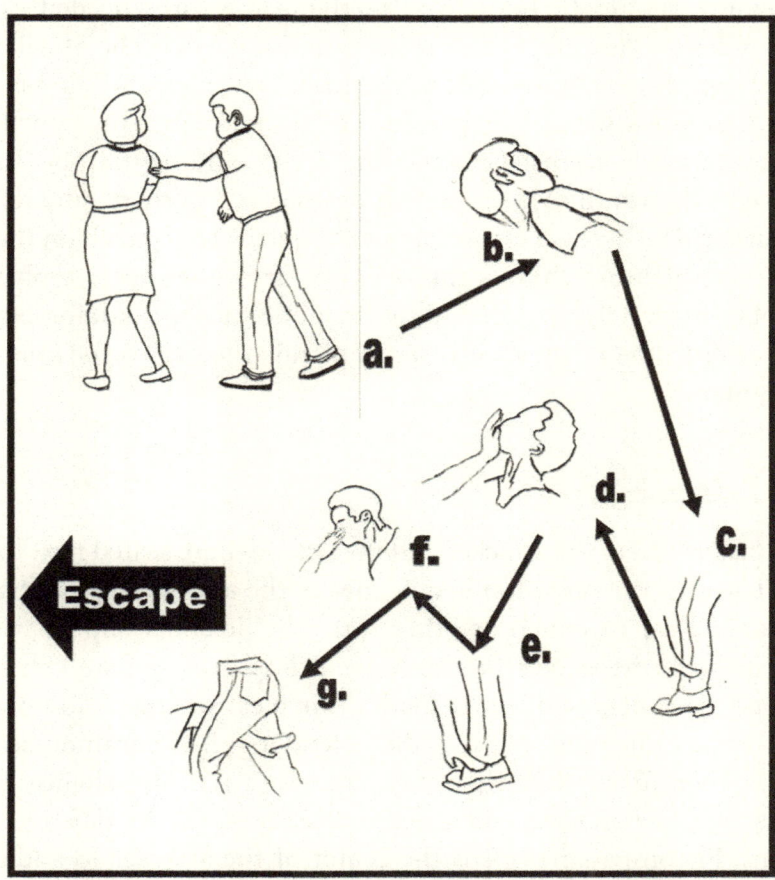

Figure 8: Grab to Back of Arm

If the defender is taller than the defender a good strike to use is an upward palm heel strike to the nose, lips, and chin of the attacker. A gouge to the eyes is also good for a smaller defender. The nurturer should read the discussion on strikes to the eye to understand how it is done and why a nurturer can do it without worry.

Follow up the initial strike with the up down shocking method alternately striking the face and feet and legs. Once distracted a side kick to one of the knees will take the attacker down long enough to make an escape.

The nurturer might hesitate in applying the force needed quickly in this defensive routine. The question to ask is why. The attacker has violated her space. The attacker has touched her. The attacker has committed a minor assault. The attacker has restricted her movement and freedom. In a self defense class the nurturer would be told to, *Get over it!* None of the routines given in this defense will permanently damage the attacker. The defense can be better compared to a smack on the bottom for a recalcitrant child. If this does not strengthen your resolve then remember most religions council to discipline such a child, for example in the letter to the Hebrews it is recommended to, *stiffen the limp hand in such matters.*

Seated Attack

This attack is where the attacker and the defender are seated next to each other. The attacker turns to the defender in the attack. This can happen in a stopped car or couch or other seat. The defender shocks with an elbow strike to the face or throat. A neck chop or ridge hand strike are also good for shocking. If the defender is in a car she needs to unbuckle the safety belt after the shock. If the defender is in a common seat she needs to slide forward and place her feet in a position slightly facing her attacker. The attacker will attempt to encompass the defender with his arms. Encompassing opens the center of the attacker to additional strikes, so the defender should take advantage of the opening.

The defender uses multiple strikes to the face, palm strikes, gouges eyes, slaps the ears, and strikes the throat. The strikes should come from as low as possible in an upward manner using a twisting movement pushing off on the floor with the feet to get as much power as possible. The defender however, is in a difficult position so when the multiple strikes are finished she must have broken out of the encompassing. There are several methods that are available. The defender can reach across her body to grab one hand by the little finger and then twisting it toward the center while raising it above her head. Using the other hand the defender can first undue the attacker's seat belt and then push on the back of the elbow to cause the attacker to bend forward. If the bending is done with vigor then the defender can cause the face of the attacker to strike the steering wheel or dash unless prevented by the safety belt. This is a complicated routine because of the restricted space in which it occurs.

The problem is that the defender has both hands involved and needs to exit the car. If the door is locked it may require some concentration and detail to exiting. This is still a dangerous situation because of the small space for the defender to work within. This is no time for the nurturer to worry about striking the eyes or throat. The attacker must be distracted for a period of about 5 seconds to make an escape out of the car. The defender can also grab the ears or the jaw and back of the head to twist the head. Holding the ears with the fingernails is probably the best option. At this point the defender backs away and stands up or steps out of the car and runs.

Keep your doors locked so someone does not enter your car that you do not want to enter. If you are a passenger in a moving vehicle turning the car off may have unintended consequences. Most modern cars lock their steering when the key is removed. Not having control of the steering is an invitation to an automobile accident. However you do not want the attacker able to drive off after your escape. This can be done by twisting the key to the start position hand holding it there while the car is moving for 5 to 10 seconds. Generally this procedure burns up the starter motor and once the car is stopped and turned off it cannot be started again without maintenance. Once stopped, the car can be turned off and the defender can do what is necessary to exit and run.

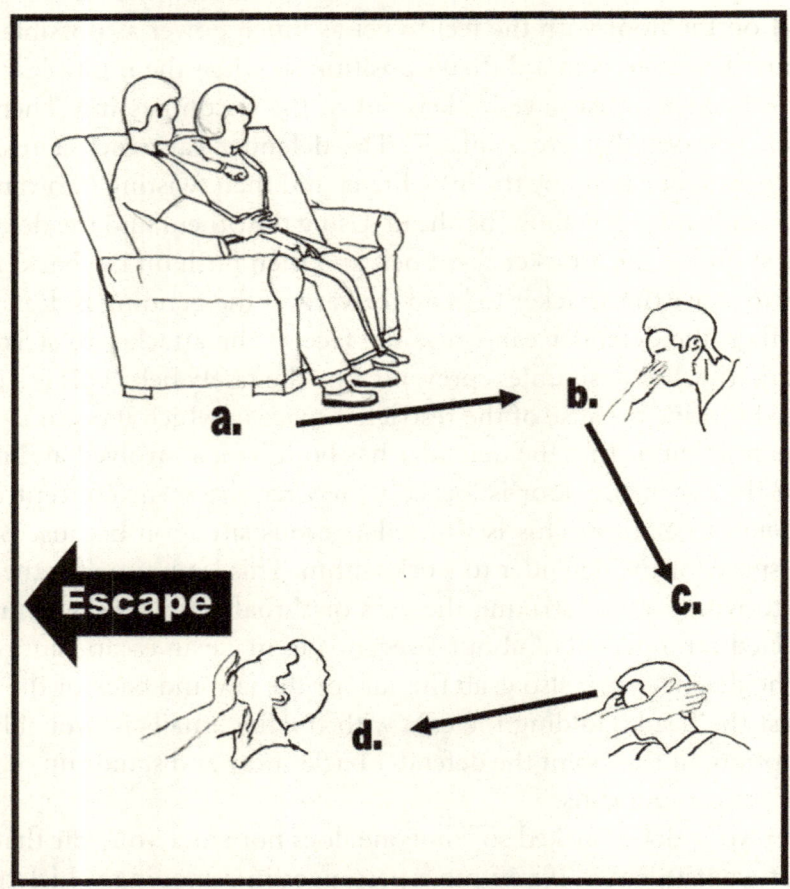

Figure 9: Seated Attack

The attacks given in this section only represent a few of the many available attacks. In Appendix A many more attacks are given, but these few can give you a defense to many common attacks. They were chosen based on requests from women taking self defense over many years of teaching.

5.

Your Position in the Village

You are strong. People look up to you. You may debate these two statements but even the abused wife that is completely dominated by an abusive husband is looked up to by her children and the dog. Now you do not want to disappoint those that look up to you to protect them from the bear. This is the place where your courage comes from in any situation. Others depend upon you and to keep them safe you have to throw yourself into the job of defense. This is a primal instinct. The *cleaving to thy husband* no matter what is not primal it is social and learned behavior. Learning to use the primal instinct is situational. If you are to the side or away when the bear goes after those you protect then you do not feel the primal urge. If you are between the bear and those you protect then you feel the primal urge. Soldiers are trained to place themselves physically in front of their buddies when there is a sign of danger and once there they rely on their training. In this situation the primal instinct can well up and you can slip into the routines you have learned and easily and face down the bear.

Above we said protecting your buddies or loved ones is a place where primal instinct kicks in. The key to this is the phrase *in any situation*. How can the casual reader of this book react to any possible self defense situation? Even masters that have studied self defense for years encounter situations that are unusual. So how do we prepare for everything?

The answer lies in the very basics of the martial art itself. In this section we will discuss the philosophical aspects of self defense. If you understand the nuts and bolts of self defense then it is easier to adapt to any situation. This will make you more powerful.

Understanding Yourself

Keep It Simple Stupid (KISS)

The primary rule for self defense is to keep the counter used to the simplest possible counter. (A counter is a set of techniques used against an attack.) This is because unless you practice complex routines carefully and often so your hands feet and body move like lightening you will probably not do the technique correctly and find yourself in worse trouble than had you not done the technique. This is particularly evident in using kicks that are higher than the belt. For example a kick that goes high takes longer and is easier to grab. Some very complex routines that throw or pin the attacker are very elegant but require endless practice. The complex blocking and striking that is done in a lightning fast manner in a Kung Fu movie is just that a routine that has been practiced for hours filmed and edited so that it looks good.

The general routine used here is:

1). *Relax*: & *become a Vessel*: Take a breath and get ready

2). *Daze*: Shock the attacker by screaming, kicking, gouging, and hitting everything in sight,

3). *Channel Your Assets*: Escape any holds usually by twisting or rotating,

4). *Harmonize*: Understand your antagonist physically and mentally,

5). *Echo, Echo, And Then Run*: Keep the counters going until you can run

To support this approach given below are descriptions of the various weapons you have available with an emphasis on the simplest approach.

Using the Hands

The picture below shows several hand positions. These positions are the result of natural nurturing movements for all humans. These movements will seem natural to women. The list of positions is as follows: a.) praising hand, b.) butterfly hands, c.) guiding hand, d.) spearing hand, e.) offering hands, f.) picking hand, g.) praying hands, h.) climbing hands (yin yang hands), and i.) petting hands. When the defender needs to grapple with the attacker the hands and fingers she uses will naturally assume one of these positions prior to the grapple.

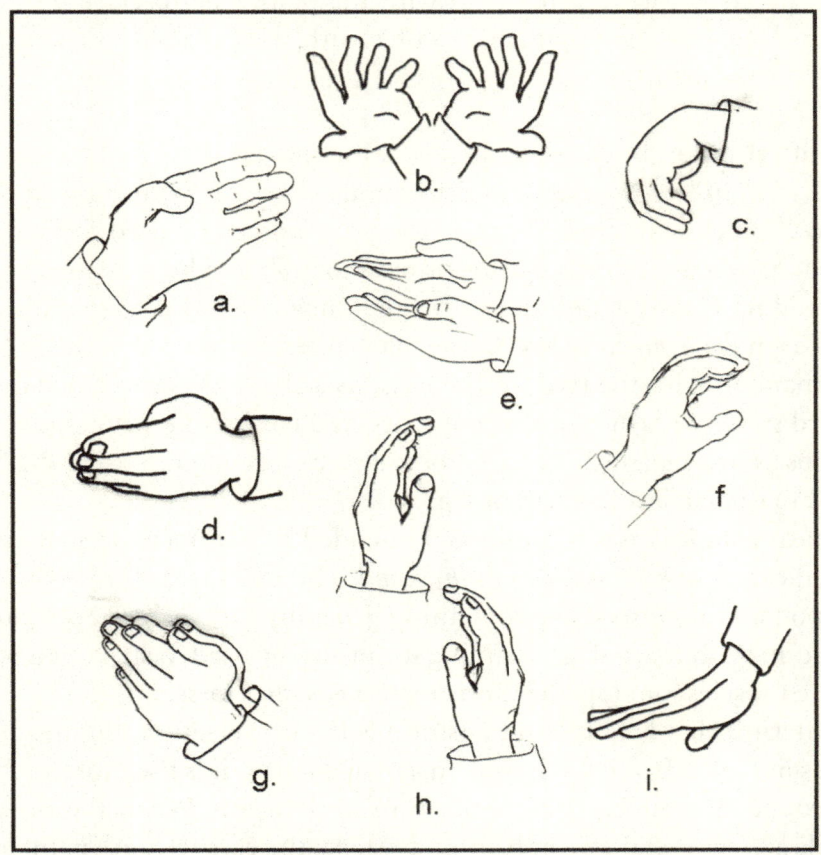

Figure 10: The Nurturing Hands

Praising Hand: A praising hand is raised as follows: The speaker at a dinner in his speech says something like *I now have the pleasure to introduce Mr. X.* At this point he raises his hand upward in a in a circular fashion placing it behind Mr. X. When this hand position is used in a martial sense there are various applications.

1. Strike a leading arm with the back of it to open the opponent's center.
2. Strike upward striking thumb and forefinger edge of the hand (a ridge hand) to lift the leading arm.
3. Strike with the chopping edge of the hand as in a neck chop.
4. Strike the leading hand with the palm side to close the hand against the opponent's center with the capability of grabbing the arm.

Butterfly Hands: Butterfly hands is the universal symbol for *no, not correct or I did not see that.* Butterfly hands are made by making an open hand X block with crossed arms. The position can be used to block an attack between the crossed arms or used to grab and hold an arm or leg.

Guiding Hands: Guiding hand is the universal soft directional shove such as in *Go away little boy.* In the martial sense it is used in the following manner: with the back of the wrist as a shove in some direction, as a hard strike with the back of the wrist, as a hard strike with closed fingertips as in an Eagle Beak strike, or as in a hook and grab using the bent hand to catch a leading arm or leg.

Spear Hand: This is the universal extended hand for a hand shake used to indicate *I have no weapon in my hand.* The striking finger tips are the weapon and used to strike something generally soft such as eyes, throat or groin. With martial arts training it can also be used to strike at a point where muscles join together and create a *Charlie Horse.*

Offering Hand: This hand position is the universal symbol for offering as in *I am offering this to you.* In a martial sense it is used for grabbing an extended arm, leg or weapon from underneath. When the offering hands are cupped they can be used to strike the ears to cause pain and a ringing in the ears.

Picking Hand: Picking hand is used in the universal sense to pick fruit but also it is used in a compare mine to yours sense. When two people are having a heated discussion at some point of discussion you will see the hand made in this position when that particular individual senses an attack on their intellectual position. The martial aspect of the hand usage is to grab something as if you are grabbing fruit. The hand position can also be used with the finger tips in a raking motion as in the Bear Claw strike. The Bear Claw strike is good for striking at the face and eyes. The picking hand when closed becomes a fist. The fist is rarely used in women's self defense. Making and using fist for strikes requires practice. The fist for good power must to be square in shape and very often the finger lengths of a woman's hand do not support a square shaped fist. The fist is not a natural and nurturing use of the hand. There are several other fists like strikes that are easily done and work well with the shape of women's hands, see the appendix on terminology.

Praying Hands: This is the universal symbol for an indication of obedience to the person to which it is offered as in a declaration of peace used in the Far East or as praying in the Western World. When the hands are shoved straight forward they can be used to spread the attacking arms apart or to strike with both sets of finger tips at the same time.

Climbing Hands: When someone is climbing the hands move in a one two manner to pull yourself upward. The lower hand supports while the upper hand reaches for more. As the person moves upward the hands reverse their roles. In martial arts the hands in this position are called Yin Yang. The Yin Yang sense comes from pulling and pushing, giving and taking which is a sense of opposites. When the hands are in this position they can be used to block or lead away an attack that is high or low with the hand that is nearest to the attack. In women's self defense they can be done without giving away the sense to your opponent that you have prepared for an attack by the *Earring Fiddle*. By using one hand to casually fiddle with your earring and the other to rest on your belt you can assume a defensive position without an obvious setting of such a stance.

Petting Hands: When someone is dealing with a dog or child, the hand is used in this manner generally with a responsive command such as, *Good Little Dog*. It can also be used with the command *Down Boy*. Petting hand is the palm heel strike or a push block.

The palm heel strike is the primary self defense strike for women. Generally this is for two reasons: 1) the different lengths of women's fingers are sometimes such that a square fist is difficult to make, and 2) women that have long finger nails cannot make a fist. The palm heel strike also has the advantage that there is only one joint between the shoulder and the striking surface so a more powerful strike can be delivered.

The push block is the most natural of the blocks and therefore the easiest block to make. It must however be delivered with the palm of the hand or the result can be jammed fingers.

Finally, there are other hand positions that come to mind such as the fist. These are generally just the continuation of these basic positions. The fist for example is just a completion of the picking hand.

Stances

Stances are fundamental to all martial arts. The placement of the feet determines if you are solid and able to support strong upper body work or flexible and able to move and change positions quickly. A great deal of work is done on stances because they provide the foundation for much of what is done. However, to the untrained or lightly trained the stances are simple in that keeping the feet wide apart when doing upper body work and close together when moving, or kicking. If the reader were to spend time in martial arts the work on stances would provide significant help in doing the techniques in this book, but the basic rule of wide or close together can get most people through what is needed.

Blocks

Blocks deflect or parry an attacking hand or foot. The block can be directed to push the attacking hand away from its intended target or to stop the attacking hand. The latter is not generally recommended for a defender that is lighter weight than the attacker. This type of block is used in some cases such as an X block to stop an attack with a knife allowing you to trap the hand. As the strike comes and is caught in the block the defender generally slips backward because the block is overcome. In this case the emphasis is on capturing the hand with the knife and not so much stopping the forward motion of the attack.

The general description given in martial arts classes of the parrying kind of block is that of crossing a stream. As you cross the water pushes you down stream deflecting you from your intended place on the opposite shore. Applied in self defense a punch comes at the defender's face and is pushed to the side with only a fraction of the force of the punch. The K.I.S.S. principle then is to simply push the attacking hand or foot to one side and don't be inventive.

Available weapons means they must be available. People rarely go about their day with a weapon hanging off of their side. That is the good news and bad news about weapons. It means a trip to the restaurant does not erupt into a gun or sword fight. However if you are depending on some weapon in your purse you will most likely never get it out in time. That means the weapons you have readily available are your best weapons. These are your hands and feet.

Other Weapons

What is in Your Hand?

Weapons are always hard to retrieve in time, so make what ever you have in your hand a weapon. This is the Jackie Chan approach. A book or rolled up news paper can be used to strike soft spots by jamming the end into those spots. Soft spots are: eyes with the corner of the book, throat with the end, bridge of the nose, up into the nose, and swung into the groin. Be creative and you will find many weapons readily available.

Pepper Spray

Pepper spray can be obtained at most hardware and auto stores. There are several cautions about pepper spray but if you need protection tonight then get some. It will take time to absorb what is in this book and if you need protection tonight then use it. The cautions are as follows.

If you are in a closed car with the pepper spray in your purse and it some how turns on you, you are in trouble. You cannot take it on most public transportation. It must be sprayed directly into the eyes and within about 3 feet. But the biggest problem is it ends up generally in the bottom of your purse for you to dig out and that is exactly where it is when you need it the most. There are also many places where you cannot take such sprays. Such sprays have security locks to prevent it from going off in your purse or at a time when not intended, but any mechanical device is not fool proof. The security device makes it something you have to understand to use. If you must use such a device then buy two and practice with one. Do such practice outside in the open air against a tree or some other target

Keys, Pencil

Keys or a pencil if they are in your hand or readily available provide a good weapon to jam into someone's hand to extract from a grip. You can jam them into an arm leg, face, eye, groin or neck. All of these will distract the attacker. If however, they are not readily available then they are of little use.

Umbrella, Cane, Flashlight

The umbrella, cane, and flashlight can all be used to strike as well as entangle the opponent. One of the problems with these weapons is that without training they can be taken away and used against you. The umbrella and cane can be used to hook the leg and pull the attacker off balance. The umbrella can be opened and placed in front of the attacker as a barrier allowing escape. These techniques require training and practice and again you must have them available to use when attacked. Canes were reasonable self defense weapons in the 19th and early 20th century when they were in vogue for style but now they are only used by the feeble and you are sending the predator the wrong signal.

Belt, Scarf, Nylons

The belt, scarf, and nylons are items that can be used as striking objects or things to entangle. The belt buckle when swung is a good stand off weapon. The same with a scarf or nylons with some heavy object in then used to swing at the opponent. The problem with all of these weapons is that they can be grabbed and used against the defender.

Shoes

The shoes can be used like a hammer to strike at a gripping hand or the face of the attacker. If the shoes do not allow the defender to run they are only good to hit the opponent. If you have to run you will have to do the running bare foot anyway.

Hand Bags

Hand bags can be used to swing if they are heavy with a long handle. A bag with a long handle can be used to entangle the opponent. They can be used as an obstruction if they are large. The small opera purse can be used like brass knuckles by gripping the metal opening clasp with your fist. All of these techniques are subject to the defender trying them out to know how well they work.

Attitude

This is the best weapon to use. Stand up straight, walk in a business like manner and do not look right or left but be aware of what is there. If someone is in your way then walk around them with an air of disdain. If there are taunting remarks then roll your eyes upward and shake your head and keep going as if you are hearing some middle school kid exploring the limits of what is acceptable to say. Once you are through the difficult area turn and make note of the entire situation including descriptions, license plates, and other data so that if there is a problem you can be a good witness for the police.

6.

Going Out to Meet the Bear

As the defending woman is alerted to the bear she gets up from grinding corn or weaving thatch and goes out to meet the bear. She automatically grasps the spear or other weapon without thought and without looking but with a plan. All of the women come out together ready and alert with the knowledge of the nature of things, and of bears.

The nature of self defense is based on the principle that all men are basically the same with two arms and two legs meaning the attacks they can execute are limited. This section provides a set of principles for self defense based on those limitations. The concepts are taken from the general instruction on self defense and often placed in language which is obscure. To make these concepts easier and more comfortable for individuals with a higher instinct for nurturing the emphasis is has been placed in nurturing terms.

The physical structure of a man also provides the keys for specific techniques for use in self defense. The structure of man determines his motion, stepping, jumping, and turning. The structure determines what position he must be in to deliver powerful strikes and apply force. The joints also provide a set of points on the body that can be used in self defense.

There is an additional principle in that if an attack is conceived by man therefore it can be overcome by man. We all think similarly. When all of these basic concepts are rolled into a system of techniques, it gives us what we need for self defense.

There is a recipe or method for self defense, sometimes called the Five Principles of Self Defense. The recipe can be broken down into specific steps. Each of these steps is discussed in an overview and then later related in practical terms for use in self defense. The recipe was given and demonstrated earlier and is worth repeating.

1). *Relax*: & *become a Vessel*: Take a breath and get ready

2). *Daze*: Shock the attacker by screaming, kicking, gouging, and hitting everything in sight,

3). *Channel Your Assets*: Escape any holds usually by twisting or rotating,

4). *Harmonize*: Understand your antagonist physically and mentally,

5). *Echo, Echo, And Then Run*: Keep the counters going until you can run

Relax & Become a Vessel

This total time for the student to perform the tasks in this section in the midst of self defense is one to two seconds. Although there is a lengthy explanation, you must be able to do the tasks required almost instantly.

Relax:

This is the first step in self defense and is to relax and initially not struggle against the attack. This is a hard thing to do. When someone grabs at you the instinct is to pull away, but this is the wrong thing to do. To not resist the student must have good mind and body control. If the attacker grabs your wrist and you pull back the grip becomes tighter. If you relax the attacker assumes he has control and the grip becomes less tight.

As an attack comes the defender must sense the nature of the attack and not resist it. When the opponent grabs, punches, or kicks, do not stand and try to absorb the energy of the attack but lead it away allowing it to glance off or direct it to a place to defeat the opponent. To use this principle the senses must be heightened. When the opponent has hold of your wrist try to sense the direction in which the opponent wants to go with your wrist. This will determine your counterattack.

It is important to assume a calm mental attitude and a relaxed stance. Do not look into the opponent's eyes and freeze. Look directly into the opponent's eyes while seeing the whole of the body and the environment around you maintaining a calm composure. The eyes are but one component of the picture. The entire picture is needed: the place it occurs, the possible escape routes, possible weapons, other potential attackers.

In the philosophical sense this principle has two levels the mental focus. The focus on the action at hand the *inner focus* and mental focus on the environment that surrounds the individual the *outer focus*. The inner focus determines the strengths of the opponent, the type of attack and its likely progression and the options for a defense. The outer focus determines if there are other opponents, the location of the escape, the amount of room, potential weapons, and other questions. All of this is good to say but how can the novice practice such a thing?

The development of an outer focus can be done by going to some public building or museum that you normally do not use. As you walk from room to room walk out to the middle of the room close your eyes and quickly mentally go over this check list: 1) where are the exits that I can use, 2) where are the large bulky furniture and barrier items that will impede me or an attacker, 3) what items are laying around that can be picked up and used and, 4) what items do I have and are wearing that I can use or will impede me? All of this must be done in the beginning in the time you can say *Mary had a little lamb*, and later in the time it takes you to say *Mary had*. After you have practiced this a couple of times you will find it easy and you will do it without thinking of it.

When the individual develops a total awareness in all directions he has developed an outer focus. Everyone has used this capability when they sensed someone or something behind them without an alert by the normal senses (sound, air motion, light changes). The student practices this with kicks and punches at a target when blindfolded. Another practice is to spar with multiple opponents which is slightly opposed to concentration for if you are totally focused on what is in front of you it becomes harder to sense what is behind.

The object of the practice is to prepare for a real situation. For example, you are drawn into a self defense situation and you remain calm and focused on the task at hand but you have in your mind an overview of your environment as if detached from yourself and are aware of potential escape routes, walls and other limitations, potential weapons, and other potential adversaries.

The development of an inner focus is not as easily practiced for you need another person to practice it with adults, child or pet. When you shake hands is there motion: what is the direction, is there sweating, how does the skin feel, is there strength and where is the strength in the fingers or in the thumb? When you get a tug on the sleeve what is the direction and urgency? When you get a nose nudging you leg did you feel the whiskers? Learn to feel those that touch you and to understand something of their intent. The religious individual that shakes your hand using two hands a petting hand and a serving hand. In this case the hand is rotated until your palm is up sandwiched between his two hands. Is he naturally fatherly? Is it real or false? The individual that shakes your hand placing his palm down gives a sense of superiority and control, is the intent to put you down or is it an unconscious striving for power over others? What happens when you force him to switch rolls by rotating your hand to the superior position?

When the individual focuses on the self defense situation at hand she must become calm. If the student is free of emotion then she is free to center on the task at hand. A person first notices the concept of inner focus when doing some task where there is a sense of slow motion. Students that have learned to focus their attention in this manner are capable of hearing and seeing more and then moving faster and more powerfully to counter the attack.

Become a Vessel or *Get It Together Girl*

The second part of this step in the recipe for self defense is to summon your energy for the upcoming struggle. *Getting it together* is the common expression for a complex philosophical notion but it is what they tell you when are talking to someone with not too much sympathy. To discuss both of these concepts we refer to this as becoming a vessel.

The oriental philosophic notion is called Capturing Ki or Chi: Chi is said to flow in simple lines into the hands and through the arms into a spot about 3 inches in diameter just below the navel. This spot is the center of gravity of the body, and the point where the major organs and major muscle groups directly or indirectly connects. It is said that it is the place where newborn baby's receive nourishment and because of that a place of residual energy for the adult. Chi is said to flow to and from all living things.

The weak and old are said capable of sucking out your Chi while children exude or give you Chi. If you go into an old age home and feel tired after you come out and you did not do anything to tire you then you lost your Chi to some needy person. The person who is in an accident and performs a feat he is unable to perform under normal circumstances, for example lifting a heavy object from someone, has captured Chi and is using it. Of course he may have had an adrenalin rush.

The first exercise practiced by the self defense student in self defense class is called *Live Hand*. One student is directed to hold another student's wrist as tight as possible. The student that is grabbed is then directed to open the fingers of the held hand as wide as possible. Both students at this point notice the strength and hardness that appears in the wrist. This method of opening the hand is used to extract the wrist when adding to it a twisting, pushing or pulling motion. Also for the student with the fingers open it is easy to grab the passing arm or leg for use in a later self defense technique.

Energy comes in many forms with components of mass, velocity, frequency of vibration, temperature, current, resistance and charge. Capturing energy is not a valid concept. The actual concept is more re-directing the energy or changing it into a different form. It comes on many levels and it is best taught by a master. It is not the exclusive province of masters. In general the concept of capturing Chi is the process of getting ready for the fight, summing your adrenalin, and making the mental decision that this must be done. Everyone has done this at some time, it is the instance when you are very tired but you have some chore that must be done before you can relax. From somewhere in the depths you get the energy to do the task. You have summoned Chi. The trick is to tap into that well of energy when you need it.

Daze or Shock

The entire process of getting it together or summing Chi must be done in a split second and follows a survey of the surroundings and the opponent, the threat, routes of escape and the amount of danger you are in. Immediately after this assessment you need to shock your opponent. To do this you fly into action rapidly striking the face, eyes, and ears with the hands while kicking the legs and feet and groin. The point of dazing or shocking your opponent is to distract him long enough to make your escape or set him up for further defensive moves so you can escape.

There are several striking recipes that are used by various martial artists. The one I have found most useful in teaching in women's self defense classes is the high-low method. I developed this method in watching and talking with women in self defense classes as well as the volunteer opponents used as attackers. After reviewing various practice sessions it is apparent that the students that stuck to this approach had the best results not because it is more powerful or more focused but because it is easy to remember and master by the novice. Strike high with say a palm strike to the face a couple of times rapidly, strike low with the feet a couple of times rapidly with say kicks to the shin, strike high again with a different strike, strike low with a different strike, and so on. There are no specific strikes or sequences but the simple rule is to strike several times what ever you see that is open. The opening is created high by striking low and vice versa.

If the attacker is very large in comparison to the defender, or if there are multiple attackers, or if the attacker has a weapon then the defender must develop a terrible resolve. In Japanese this is *Hidoi Sabaki* and is something similar to a death wish. When the attack on Pearl Harbor was over the Japanese Admiral Yamamoto remarked that he was afraid *we have awakened a sleeping giant and given it a terrible resolve*. This is the mental quality the defender must have for she is required to fling herself into the task to survive. The problem with this is that women are nurturers and reluctant to hurt or injure anyone, which is exactly what they need to do. Injury comes in degrees and it is highly unlikely that a 120 pound woman can severely injure a 250 pound man unless she has had considerable training. However she must develop the resolve if necessary to escape, to stick a thumb nail in his eye or hit him with an object when he drops to one knee and not feel guilty about it. The justification that you need to remember is that for anyone that is large to attack someone that is small makes him by his actions a bad guy.

As a guy I confess I am never around when I am needed. We had a sick cat. I could not be home because of my job until 2PM. I had suggested to my wife that she wait until then to take the cat to the vet to be put down. I called shortly before 2PM to find that she had already taken the cat to the vet. There was deadness in her voice. It was the sound of the terrible resolve. She had done what I could not. She had developed the resolve to end the pain of the small creature as soon as possible with whatever was needed. She used this resolve to drive the creature in the car for the half an hour to the vet and the half an hour back with the empty cat box in the back seat. Later she allowed the sadness to set in. This is a terrible resolve. It can be used in what I call the method actor's application to self-defense. Recall some time in your life when you have had this feeling. Learn to summon up that feeling at will then direct it at your antagonist.

The process of shocking the opponent is taking the captured energy of the opponent's attack and redirecting it back to the opponent added to your own. This allows you to shock your opponent. Often the result is rapid staccato like strikes. This is not always the case for shocking the opponent. It may also mean a rapid throw or other technique the opponent is not expecting. Summoning your Chi and shocking your opponent depends upon establishing roles and distances. In the case of a charging opponent, summoning your Chi may mean redirecting his energy to the floor with a trip or throw. In any case at the end the opponent should be dazed. This daze will allow you to use other assets you have to escape.

Channeling

Channeling: Channeling is the nurturer's word for the physical concept of choreographing or directing. The principle of channeling has its basis in the idea that to stop a thing in motion interferes with the nature of it whereas redirecting its motion does not attempt to fundamentally alter the nature of it. In the western world this is represented by Newton's laws of motion. In other words movement makes the object committed to a particular path. The kick or strike that commits to a motion which is straight forward cannot suddenly be changed to some other motion halfway through the kick or strike.

In oriental philosophical terms the principle of channeling is the "Water Principle". The student is told to imagine walking across a fast moving stream. As his foot is put into the water it tends to push on him in the direction of the flow of the water. As he walks across the stream he is deflected down stream. A fist moving forward can be deflected much easier by pushing it to the side rather than stopping it by pushing directly against is motion. The pushing to the side always results in a circular motion. Pulling along the motion will add the momentum of the opponent's body to the process allowing it use in other techniques. The rapid or slow movement of the defender in big or small circles allows the application of self defense techniques. It is important to bring the defense in a continuous manner, flowing from one technique to another until there is an opportunity for escape. For the nurturer this is similar to choreographing a dance. By combining the continuous defense with circular motion the attacker is faced with an ever changing target and must continuously adjust his attack.

These are pretty words but how does the novice apply such a thing? Picture the ice skaters all in a row skating around in a circle. The one at the center does little skating while the one on the outer end of the line must skate very fast. A man grabbing the sleeve of your blouse can be dislodged by spinning around. This motion is just as if the defender is the center skater. Now picture the same line of skaters where the outer skater, for example a clown, hits the barrel and goes tumbling. As you spin around to dislodge the attacker deliver a strike with your hand or forearm to the face.

Someone grabs your shoulders from behind. Extend your arms and spin around striking towards the face. The angular momentum of the spinning body will always exceed the ability of the hands to hold onto the shoulders. If you are car jacked turn your wheels as far as you can and jam the accelerator to the floor, provided there is room to do such a thing. First it is hard to hit a moving target and a heavy spinning thing becomes dangerous.

Harmonizing

To harmonize is the nurturing equivalent of the oriental philosophical concept of *Becoming One*. In the diagram above the there are four physical positions of harmony a.) to d.) and mental harmony, e.) If you harmonize yourself with the opponent completely then any attack will in effect be negated because you shift mentally and physically to maintain the harmony. If in the process of the attacker launching an attack toward you, you the defender, have added some of your force to the attacking technique then the result will generally be to the detriment of the opponent. Consider the following attack. An attacker uses both hands to grab the defender's lapels. The defending student grabs the attacker's lapels, steps and tusrns holding the lapels placing his back directly against the opponent. At this point the student becomes one with the opponent. The attacker is now in a throwing position. In almost every throw the student will end in the same physical location and position as the attacker started in when the throw is successfully done.

The next level of sophistication in the concept of harmonizing or becoming one with the opponent is to channel his motion. This is to naturally blend with his motion or attack to deflect it and become your counterattack. This may also involve the concept of adherence.

Adherence is sticking to the opponent during motion. Adherence will lead to situations where the opponent is off balance and allow you to cause him to fall.

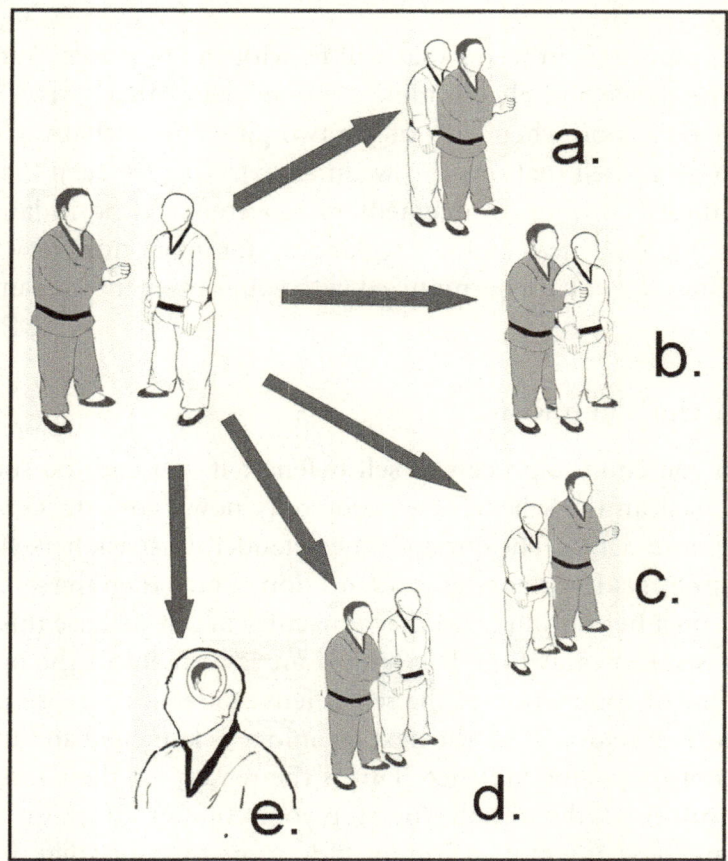

Figure 11: To Harmonize

The final level of sophistication is to harmonize or become one with the mental attitude of the opponent and to know your opponents next action because you are in tune with his mind. These are the three levels of becoming one with the opponent.

Again, these are pretty concepts but what good is it for the female novice. You know how your mother always inexplicably knew when you did something wrong. This was true so much that she could say, *I know what you've been up to*, and you felt guilty whether or not you were up to anything.

Let us place this in terms that will fit with the nurturer. Young girls have done dance and cheerleading routines with other girls. The routines get very good when each of the two girls know what the other is going to do so well that one throws in an extra step or turn the second follows directly with a complementary movement. If both dancers are contributing new ideas and not seeking to dominate then very creative steps follow. If you have harmonized with your opponent the same effect occurs.

Echo, Echo Then Run

How do you end the process of self defense? If you end too soon then you are back in the self defense mode only now your attacker is wary and harder to defeat. The question the defender must ask herself is *can I make my escape*? If the answer is no or I don't know then the self defense process must be continued. In the vernacular of self defense this mental process is called escalation. It is simply an assessment of the opponent at the time of completion of the self defense to see if more is needed to assure he is subdued. If so, the next technique is launched and this technique is of increasing violence. This is the reason for the name escalation. If you think the minute you stop your counter attack the attacker will again come at you then you must do more to assure that this is not the case.

For example, upon completion of the block of a punch and turn to an elbow strike, the defender looks to see if the attacker is subdued. If he is not subdued then there is a back fist and so on with the violence increasing with each technique. A new set of techniques are done and again the assessment is made. In computer programming this is a "Do Loop", or an echo of the previous counters.

The wince of pain by the opponent can deflect your concentration and cause you to relax allowing another attack. Simply, the defender judges the attacker's will and ability to counter not whether he is in pain. If the attacker has not given up then continue the counters until he does not have the will to continue or until you can clearly escape. For the nurturer the comparison is with a recalcitrant child. You get bad behavior and you assign a punishment. For example the child is given *a time out*. When you get more bad behavior, you assign a tougher punishment and so on until the child decides the punishment is too great for the benefits resulting from the bad behavior. Afterward the nurturer goes into the room of the sobbing child to review what he did wrong and why you as the parent had to reprimand him. For the nurturer that is involved in an altercation and the attacker is now in court, you can leave the explanation of the reprimand he is getting to the Judge.

7.

Understanding Life in the Village

This section is to familiarize the reader with some of the philosophic concepts of self defense. These are basic concepts of living such as equilibrium, agility, pliability, focus, efficiency and others. What the reader should take away from this section is in the things done in every day life. Read this section carefully and one day as you close the drawer in the kitchen and turn to carry the main dish to the table it is as if you have pushed an attacking hand aside and turned with serving hands to quickly take control of a weapon in the attacker's hand. The smoothness of it is apparent because you are full of the qualities of equilibrium, focus and spirit as women throughout the ages.

Understanding Equilibrium & Agility

I have seen masters giving demonstrations of equilibrium, where they take a particular stance and others try to dislodge them. There are stories of a karate master that stood on the roof of his house in a horse stance during a typhoon to hold his house down. These are to inspire the student to pursue good stances. Good stances are basic, without them there is no self defense. The various stances are used for different techniques and activities.

Standing with your feet firm with the ground and wide apart allows you to do upper body work, punching, throwing, entanglements, and joint manipulation. In empty hand methods such as karate or tae kwon do these are called front stances, horse stances, or base stances. Your equilibrium is good but you give up your agility. It is hard to move in these stances so martial arts teaches the student to drop into these stances to do the upper body work and quickly change to a more mobile stance.

In stances where the feet are close together you have agility but your upper body is weaker. In empty hand methods such as Karate or Taekwondo these are called back stances, sword stances, cat stances, and cross stances. When a boxer fights he is generally in one of these stances so he can move in all directions. However, when he throws a punch the forward foot steps wide to deliver the punch and then steps quickly back. Kick boxers can quickly bring up a knee for a block in this stance but striking something with the hand while on one foot is so weak as to move the striker backward rather than the one that is hit.

Equilibrium must be maintained when shifting from one stance to another. When shifting from a front stance used for striking, a joint lock or entanglement to a back stance for sweeping or reaping take downs if there is a moment of non-equilibrium then all is lost and the advantage will quickly shift to the attacker. There is a balance between equilibrium and agility in the nature of things. In science this is Heisenberg's principle. If you know the location of something it has no movement. If you know the movement, its location is unknown to a certain extent.

For the nurturer, Mrs. Heisenberg might say *when getting the butter dish down from the top shelf dear use a wide stool to stand on or I'll know exactly where you will be, … on the floor silly.*

Understanding Pliability

The classic definition here is to pick up a noodle with chopsticks, however even the use of chop sticks appears a dieing art. In the modern world there is no direct correlation to this picture. Perhaps it relates to eating your spaghetti with a spoon without cutting it. If you completely relax when you are thrown, you can overcome the throw whereas if you struggle against it you will assist in the throw. This is the defense taught for a throw, *Become the bag of potatoes*. Become completely limp and sink downward. Sinking downward improves your ratio of center of gravity to the attacker. When you are limp the throw requires the attacker to use upper body strength totally for the throw. This may cause a loss of balance for the attacker. If you sense this loss of balance then you in turn can use this to pull the attacker off balance.

Pliability is more than utilizing limpness. It involves both the mind and body. The entire body from head to foot at times must be pliable and may in the next second be fixed, strong, focused and not pliable. The ability to rapidly shift focus is only done with a pliable mind. The self defense situation is ever changing and the defender must adapt again and again to changing situations.

Understanding Focus

Inner Focus

Inner focus is concentration. For example when you ride an elevator watching the lights of the floors waiting to get off at your floor you are only partly aware of the music that permeates the environment. This is the inner focus.

This concentration is not total, because the elevator music gets through. The inner focus you need is to feel the fingernails as they dig into the pressure point between the thumb and forefinger without looking. Inner focus is the sense in the grabbed arm that the attacker wants to pull or push in a certain direction. This focus can be improved by training. Practice at touching and feeling things that someone else manipulates can significantly improve this sense. Nurturers have more of this naturally than those that are non-nurturers. Petting the cat and feeling a bump on her skin is a natural thing for the nurturer.

Inner focus causes the tingle in the back of your neck when someone is behind you; the limit causes your nostrils to flair at a wafting smell, or the feeling of the bead of sweat on your forehead at the slightest change in air temperature around you. These senses come from deep primal spots in your memory. You can train to improve these senses and they become very useful. That cat you have just petted, can you sense it walking behind the couch if it is not making clearly audible noise. It stops and stands up on two feet. Do you know what it is about before it sharpens its claws on the back of the couch or do you hear the noise and then realize you knew before it was done..

Outer Focus

When you look at a distant object with binoculars you adjust the focus until it becomes clear. If you move your gaze slightly to an object at a different distance you must again adjust the focus. In self defense you focus on many things, the movement of the shoulders, the quick glance of the eyes, the tightening or slackening of the grip, and the reaction to your defensive technique, all of which may occur in two or three seconds. Your focus must shift and shift again but be clear and precise when it is focused on some part of the activity. This is sometimes called the outer focus.

The shifting of focus is important. Take the example of a deer eating grass beside the road at night. She is totally focused on getting a good mouthful of tasty grass. Suddenly she sees is in the light that just appeared patch of tasty grass just across the road. She is totally focused on the grass as she walks across the road which accounts for the surprised look just before she encounters the hood of the Honda.

If you are in a place with a single exit then when you finish the self defense against an opponent or opponents then you are in a place to quickly exit, not at the other end where you would need to step over your opponents to leave. When you are aware of the exit and intend on using it you will move in a manner that will alert the watching predator to be wary. In a proper use of outer focus such an action occurs naturally without planning, without consideration, without loss of inner focus to achieve the result.

Mental Attitudes

Having a clear and focused mind is essential to self defense. Every one has experienced and used the techniques necessary. The child catches its hand in the door. You quickly extract it. You examine it. You decide what aid is needed and see to it. After you have done all of these tasks you comfort, nurture and sooth. You may fall all apart when you imagine in your mind it happening to the child's hand, but for a moment you were all business. This attitude of calmness is what you need to nurture in yourself. When faced with a self defense situation do what is necessary then when you get home away from others over a hot cup of tea, then you can fall apart. This quick taking charge and returning to a calm attitude is the antithesis of a predator, he builds up to the point where he chases down his prey. Behaving this way when seen by a predator will make him wary.

Physical Attacks

The rule here for you to use is the *John Wayne Rule*. Any big person that picks on a smaller, frailer, older, or very young person is a bad guy, *the pick on someone your own size* rule. This is a clear decision process. You know that whatever you have to do is ok because you are dealing with a bad guy.

Now you know who you are dealing with and you know his targets. Knowing your enemy is a large part of knowing what to do. For the smaller defender the attacker will strike to intimidate. On a woman he will strike those areas that are important to her in a primal sense, her face, her belly, her hair, her clothing, and her modesty. He knows this because he is keyed into the primal, he understands it without knowing he does. He is a predator.

Verbal Attacks

Verbal attacks are about two things 1) intimidation and 2) *prep-work* for the attack. They are build-up prior to the attack. Think of it as dancing around the fire to build courage. The attacker gets in your face and uses language designed to attack your sensibilities.

He is looking for that fleeting glance, the movement backward, that indication of intimidation so he can start his attack. Generally, the attacker wants something to occur. If you can assess that, then you know what you have to do. The attacker has some grievance real or imagined that he is trying to address. If you can assess it then you will know what to do. The chances are however you will not be able to address his grievance.

There are no set responses. Sometimes turning and walking away will defuse the situation and sometimes it will set it off. Sometimes laughing at the situation will defuse the situation and sometimes it will set it off. Sometimes talking out the problem will defuse the situation and sometimes it will set it off. So what do you do? Whenever you have such a question always return to the very basis of what you are working on. For self defense this is the rule: that all men are the same regardless of education, physical attributes, mental processes, race, age and what ever else you can list. Seek to understand all men then you are able to easily estimate what the response should be. Trust your first instincts and try the approach that you think inside will work. If that does not work on the first split second then quickly shift to another. The ability to quickly adapt will disconcert the potential predator.

Fear Avoidance

In the military a large emphasis is put on preserving the unit, the team, and your fellow soldiers. It is this attitude that is used to overcome fear. *I can't let them hurt my brothers so I must climb out of this trench and charge the machine gun nest.* This is the stuff of Congressional Medal of Honor winners. Unselfishly the soldier puts himself in danger to protect others. Fear had no part in the decision. He saw what needed done and he did it to protect the team.

Who is your team, your unit? The team is the others you help, nurture, teach, feed, love, or will teach, feed or love. The team is your children, yet born children; friends or that nice looking girl that could be your friend; parents or the old people I someday will help. You are facing down a *Bad Guy* for those in your team. Self defense is not about self but about the others that the self (you) need to protect.

This will free you from fear. *I cannot let this smuck try to stop me from doing what needs to be done to help others.* The predator will sense this terrible resolve that you have just developed and hesitate and perhaps leave.

Understanding Efficiency and Quiet

Efficiency and quiet are given together here because they are linked.

Efficiency is the ratio of the effective or useful output to the total input in any system. If I were mentally to cause the attacker to trip over his own feet my input energy is small and the output energy is large, near 100%. Having a higher efficiency is better. As the student practices some techniques he will get the sense of elegance. You know the expected result. You do the technique and get the result in a manner which caused you to catch your breath. This is the sensing of a high efficiency of the routine. Efficiency is the result of doing something in a natural manner.

An example of efficiency for the nurturer might be cooking a complex meal with foods of different cooking times, multiple preparation methods in a manner such that it all comes together just at the right time with the perfect presentation on the table. Efficiency is also the nurturer caring for the baby, cleaning house, doing tasks for a volunteer effort, coordinating the carpool with the other mothers. It is efficiency or multi-tasking that works well.

Efficiency has another aspect in that when you know it is working well there is a sense of mental quietness. There can be quiet in the midst of a din of activity. There can be a din in quiet places. Quiet is a sense of the mind not a quality of the environment.

Every martial art practices meditation. Meditation can be done sitting, standing or moving. Moving meditation can be done in Tai Chi. This is the quest of quietness. There is nothing magic in meditation it is learning to control your breathing. Breathing is a natural process. It adapts itself to the needs of your body. When you finish physical activity you may find yourself panting. This is probably the result of your not breathing correctly during the physical activity and now your body is trying to compensate.

The example of breathing is given as follows. Two women are jogging. They are talking to each other as they go. Their minds are on the conversation. They are enjoying the run and they go a distance and are not too exhausted. One of them runs alone. She does not talk but concentrates on individual things in her mind. The distance run is less then when running with her friend and when she is done she is exhausted. Why does this happen? Simply because in talking as they run, the two women are breathing correctly in a natural manner.

What is the process? In talking to make a point, laughing, and singing to project air is forced out by the diaphragm. The diaphragm is a band of muscles at the bottom of the lungs that when constricted forces air out of the lungs rapidly. At the same time the muscles across the stomach get tighter and harder. This is the reason for Karate teachers instructing their students to scream when punching, blocking, and kicking.

Contrary to what some say this is not a more natural process of breathing than the shallow breathing you are doing when at low rates of activity. Your body in this case is only asking for the oxygen it needs to do the job at the time. When we fight, if our concentration on activities within the fight causes us to stop breathing at the rates the body wants for the proper amount of oxygen, then we are out of breath at the end of the activity. Therefore we train to scream using the diaphragm to force air out of our lungs knowing that it is replaced with air rich in oxygen. We train to increase our breathing during rapid periods of activity rather than having the body do a catch up at the end when it realizes there was all of this activity and now there is not enough oxygen in the blood stream.

In Lamaze, women are trained to breath in a rapid manner in order to provide lots of oxygen in the birthing process. Excess oxygen increases the sense of euphoria which helps in managing pain. Focusing on the routine and process also helps manage the birth. In a sense Lamaze is birthing meditation. In the past in martial arts professional assassins (Ninja) were trained to prepare themselves for their task by a sequence of rapid breathing and holding their breath. The breathing routine is almost identical to Lamaze. In a sense this is comparing the ultimate nurturer with the anti-nurturer, but this is forced high efficiency breathing followed by forced quiet.

We train to achieve quiet in the midst of din. This is not a natural thing to do. However with much training it becomes routine and becomes as if natural. If you can achieve quiet in this manner then your abilities in self defense are greatly increased. This is moving meditation and a step away from Mushin Museo. Mushin Museo is the oriental concept of being of no mind or to put it another way without conscious thought of a particular task. Mushin is the doing a task without thinking of the doing of it. For those nurturers that have driven a car home and cannot remember the details of the drive then they have experienced Mushin. We train to perform a series self defense movements to achieve a result without consideration or conscious thought.

Understanding the Attack

The ultimate self defense for any attack is being at some other place at the time of the attack so the attack never occurs. For this reason this part of the book covers the attack environment. When are you likely attacked and when not? To answer this question you must consider the requirements of the attacker. From Sun Tzu in the Art of War[10], *to know your enemy is to know yourself.* Or, in other words if you know your enemy well you can anticipate his will, his requirements, and his actions. Assuming the attacker is rational, he will generally not conduct the attack in an environment where he cannot escape. He will want to inhibit the escape potential of the victim. He will want to limit the ability of the victim to identify the attacker. He will want to limit the potential of the victim to summon help. If you consider these requirements in total then it paints the picture of the dark closed in area such as a subway or alley. This is the environment where an attack can occur. It is also an environment where the hair on the back of your neck stands up. Why do you get this reaction? It is an animal instinct (a sense of being hunted). These are instincts that can be relied upon. If you sense this feeling then leave the area and get to an area that is well lighted with other people. What you need to be able to do is when you get this sensation you automatically turn to face your threat with the resolve to handle it instead of a bewilderment about what is going on.

There is another quality of the attack. By committing himself to a particular attack, the attacker also opens himself to a set of counterattacks. For example, an attacker using both hands to grab the lapels has no hands available for defensive moves and opens himself to a kick or knee to the groin. This is a fundamental principle of warfare and self defense. For the attacker, be careful what you commit yourself to do, it may get you in trouble.

The following paragraphs will review several attacks. These attacks are broken down into modes of attack, common attack areas, and composure of the victim. Potential modes of attack generally come in an attack from the front, from the side, or from the rear. Attacks can come by surprise or as a result of gradual confrontation. If you realize you are in a confrontational situation it is always best to retreat and run away. Even with the attacker in possession of a gun it is best to run. Hitting a moving target is much harder than a fixed target.

Frontal Attack

The attacker has a desire to intimidate the victim as part of his need to dominate and to assure his safety. The common areas attacked to initiate the intimidation are the face and stomach. A slap or backhand to the face and a punch to the stomach are common attacks. For example, the face attack provides a psychological advantage in that women abhor face damage. The stomach attack provides a similar advantage, in that a strong strike to the stomach will knock the wind out of the victim and prevent a scream. To prepare, keep one hand high and one low in a casual approach such as appearing to fiddle with the ear or eyes or hair. Keeping one hand high allows the defender the ability to make an easy block. This position maintains a semi-fighting posture without looking aggressive. Avoid looking the attacker directly in the eyes. Look just to the right or left of the eyes so you can see the entire attacker (arms, hands, feet, legs). Appear as unconcerned as possible and ignore any taunts or insults.

Attack from the Rear

Attacks from the rear are the most dangerous attacks. In the frontal attack, the attacker is basically not sure he wants to carry the attack off or it is done at the spur of the moment. The attack from the rear shows intent to do bodily harm and a certain amount of preplanning. At the first sign of an attack from the rear every effort should be made to immediately protect the throat. The throat is the ultimate target zone from such an attack. A posture with the chin tucked downward a good first step until you can get your hands and arms in place to protect these areas. Tucking your chin will prevent you from being choked. This may mean backing into the attacker to maintain the tucked chin. There are ways thwart such an attack once you have inhibited the primary target.

Attack from the Side

Attacks from the side can be thought of as either attacks from the front or rear. An attack to the side is either a frontal attack or a rear attack depending on whether you turn into or out of the attack.

Grabs to Clothing or Other Articles

Grabbing the clothing is an attempt to slow you down. If the clothing is loose and comes off then run away. The same is true for a purse. It is an attempt to slow you down. You should keep calm and extend yourself as far from the attacker as possible preferably in a side facing position. Do not continue to pull, as it will tend to make you appear frantic to the attacker giving him courage to continue. Attacks can potentially come anywhere but common sense will tell you not to go into some situations. The clothing you wear will also help. If the clothing is so tight that you cannot kick waist high then you are severely restricted in your counter attacks.

Cautions on Biting the Attacker

For a while biting the attacker was not recommended for freeing your self because of the risk of AIDS, however now with more information on AIDS the risk is realized as small. If you are generally free of breaks in the skin or mouth sores there is little or no risk. If you are in a life-threatening situation it is the victim's decision for you can live a long time with AIDS compared to dieing in the next second or two. The recommendation is to bite anything in range if it will lead to your escape.

Understanding the Spirit of the Opponent

This is the will of the opponent. Without drugs or extreme mental conditioning the will of most men is apparent. You know it by looking at him and watching his behavior. You know this because you have dealt with other humans and can compare their actions. When you encounter someone with a will to do something without regard for his own welfare you know this inside. The trick is to learn to recognize the signs. When you meet someone with a cold uncaring and determined attitude you know he is dangerous. When you meet someone who is reckless, careless, and clumsy, you know to step back for he is an accident waiting to happen.

The inferred proposition is that your will is part of the foundation of self defense. If you have the will to fight without regard to your own safety then you increase your power. This is the concept behind the Samurai.

If you are willing to give up your life in the fight you suddenly increase your power significantly. It is however, a bridge for the spirit that not all are willing to cross. Another way to think of this is in the game of poker. If you think about the money you may loose, then you will loose. If you think of the money as only a tool to winning then you will be willing to bluff or bet or do whatever is necessary to win. You bluff by looking into your fellow player's behavior and know he will not challenge your bluff.

These actions are based on knowing the spirit of the opponent. Nurturers have a natural instinct for this. When you were younger you did something that was intended clandestine but your mother knew what you were about. This happened so much that you had the feeling that she was reading your mind. She just understood your spirit.

Understanding Thinking and Behavior

This area is divided into two parts 1) the opponent's thinking and behavior and 2) your thinking and behavior. You can use the attacker's own thinking and behavior against him. The attacker grabs and holds on to you. You relax which in turn causes him to relax his grip. When you sense the slackening of the grip you escape. This is the knowing of your opponent's mind and behavior. You get this capability by enjoying all people, by understanding them, knowing them, anticipating their behavior in small things, and then applying these comparisons to your opponent in self defense.

The second area is your thinking and behavior. Who wins in most of the contests you encounter? The answer is the confident and self-assured. It is simple then, be that person. Develop self confidence. There is only one way to accomplish this, it is to follow *The Way* and *The Way is by Training*. If you practice assiduously you can accomplish almost anything. Self confidence comes from practicing a thing so much it becomes routine.

Understanding the Attack of the Smaller

Attacking an individual that is smaller or the helpless means the attacker has committed himself to the social place in the world of a certain kind of individual. This group of individuals lashes out at someone generally unable to defend against the attack. This group of people ranges from the one that looses his temper and strikes his wife to the torturer of kittens. They are all of one group and the difference is only a matter of the choice of the target for the violence.

When a man strikes a woman with intent he has a few primary target areas: face, hair, breasts, belly, clothing, children, or what ever the woman prizes. The strike is meant to intimidate. If the intimidation does not occur the violence will escalate. Once the intimidation is achieved there may or may not be remorse, but as in all warfare the remorse is really regrouping and repositioning of your forces for the next attack. Or, for the predator example, this is the kitty cat playing with the mouse before she bites it just in the right place to kill.

Understanding the Physical Opponent

Vulnerable Points

There are many points on the human body that are vulnerable to attack. The attack can be a strike or pressure or manipulation. The vulnerable points generally fall into two classes.

The first class of vulnerable places is where a bone structure is on the other side of a delicate portion of skin, muscle, or organ and can be squeezed against the bone structure. The ear is next to the skull, grind it into the skull and there is pain. The eye is next to the skull, strike it and there is pain. The philtrum is in front of the teeth strike it and there is pain and bleeding. The range of targets covers the nose, the lower lip, the throat, the hair, the cheek skin, and so on until you cover the entire body down to the shin, ankle and toes. These places are where you can crush delicate skin to bone. The crushing can be a strike, kick, rubbing or friction burn. Places where muscles bunch together can be caused to have a "Charlie Horse" by striking with a pointed fist or knuckle when the muscles are tight.

The second class of vulnerable places is where tendons attach muscle to bone. These points occur on each side of a joint. A simple press of the fingernail can cause pain at these locations. For example, between each of the knuckles of the hand, an inch above or below the inside of the elbow, and the inside of the wrist are a few of these places. They become important in loosening the grip of the attacker or preparing him for a joint manipulation technique.

There are places where you can crush organs to these bones. For example, the primary artery in the neck carries blood to the brain. This is impeded in the classic sleeper hold, which when used properly can cause the effected person to pass out in a matter of seconds. The strike to the throat which constricts the airway can cause fainting or death.

Places where balance or motion can be disrupted. For example, a side kick to the knee when it is locked can cause the Anterior Cruciate Ligament (ACL) to tear which will cause the person a loss of mobility for a considerable time. Not a bad counter, because in court you can identify your attacker as the guy with the limp.

In the martial arts class the student is told to study all of these vulnerable points and be able to provide at least one strike or manipulation when asked.

The Joint

Because the attacker has restricted his own actions by committing to a particular attack, the basic counter to a grapple involves manipulating a joint. The joints form an easy way to characterize the many counters available into sets that become natural to apply.

The available counters to these joints come in three approaches: 1) a joint lock, 2) a joint crank, and 3) a joint fold. The remaining piece of the counter is simply to use these joint manipulations within the principles of self defense.

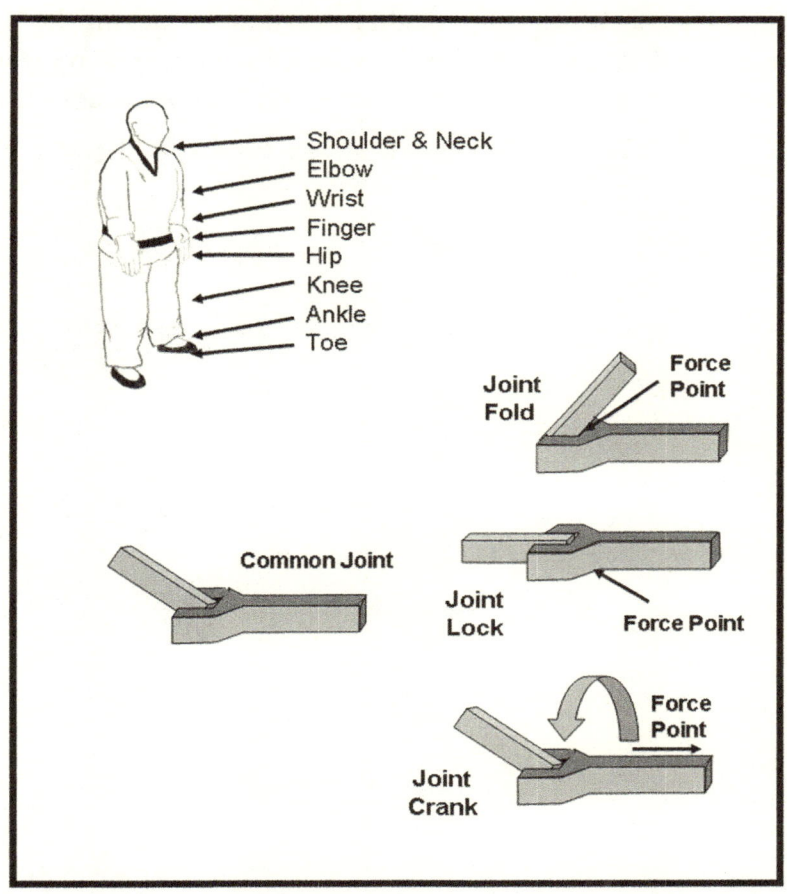

Figure 12: The Joint

To illustrate this we will use a Hand Crank to a Twist Bar counter. The attacker shoves the defender with one hand. The defender rotates away from the push to the center of the attacker grabbing the hand from the back and twisting it 180 degrees in the direction of the rotation, bending the wrist back to the limit creating a wrist crank. The arm is fully drawn out and twisted away from the outside causing an arm bar by use of the wrist crank. By continuing to twist, the twist bar force is applied across the normal motion of the wrist and by pressing down on the elbow with the other hand an arm bar is created. If the defender rotates away from the action the attacker can be brought to the floor by kicking the back of the knee. The description above technique is but once shown (generally in a martial arts school) is quick, simple, and effective against a much larger opponent.

8.

Conclusion

In writing this book there are several fundamental ideas presented. One of these ideas is the need to understand the behavior of the potential attacker. This is a natural thing for the nurturer. The best example comes from Agatha Christie. In explaining her capability at solving the crime, Miss Marple says that all she does is watch and understand people's behavior and she sees all the possible types, even in the small town of St. Mary Mead. She just extrapolates the actions of the people of St. Mary Mead to the ones she meets in the course of solving the crime she happens upon. She is the quintessential nurturer sitting on her couch solving crimes while knitting someone a shawl. Of course Agatha Christie never wrote a story that I know of where Miss Marple kicked someone in the groin and gouged him with her knitting needles but somehow it is not all that far fetched.

Another fundamental concept is that we as a species are designed essentially the same and because of this the attacks that an attacker can use will fall into a finite set that can be practiced. Adding to this the fact, the behavior is the generally something you have seen before then the attack can be anticipated. As nurturers you know this for either you have done IT as a child or seen IT as a parent or guardian. The child that is told not to do something again and they look around just before they try to do whatever IT is again. The nurturer mother is right on top of the child anticipating that they would try IT again. This is the mother's form of gotcha. We have all done this and looked up in bewilderment not knowing how she could have known we were going to try it again.

The concept of the source of courage is a tough one. Courage comes not from thinking of ones self but from thinking of someone else's well being. In this concept, a situation is instantaneously presented to you in which, to protect someone else you must put yourself in danger. This stepping into danger is done without hesitation, not because you are thinking of yourself but because you are thinking of someone that is in your nurturing family. The extrapolation is that when attacked by someone the thought occurs that *this jerk may try this on me but if I don't do something now he will try this on one of my sisters.*

A hard thing for the nurturer is shedding the worry about striking and injuring anyone even an attacker. What I have presented is in two parts. First is sorting out the bad guys from the good guys. If you have paid attention when I said that the observed behavior of some individuals can be extrapolated to other individuals then it is easy to tell the bad guys from the good ones even if you may not like the answer. Any one who picks on someone that is smaller, helpless, or weaker is a bad guy, The John Wayne Rule—*Pick on someone your own size.*

The second part of this concept is that it is very hard to do permanent injury to someone no matter what you have seen in the movies. You can stick your fingers right in the eye of someone and it is most likely that the injury is minor. With a little training the chances of injury can be made significantly less and the chances of securing your escape significantly better. So the answer for the nurturer is to look on it like an attitude correction for a recalcitrant child.

All of these concepts are rolled into the recipe for self defense. The recipe is 1). *Relax:& Become a Vessel*: Take a breath and get ready, 2). *Daze*: Shock the attacker by screaming, kicking, gouging, and hitting everything in sight, 3). *Channel Your Assets*: Escape any holds usually by twisting or rotating, 4). *Harmonize*: Understand your antagonist physically and mentally, 5). *Echo, Echo, Then Run*: continue doing the fight until you can escape escalating the violence as you continue Each of these concepts are not foreign to the nurturer, in fact they are natural nurturing concepts.

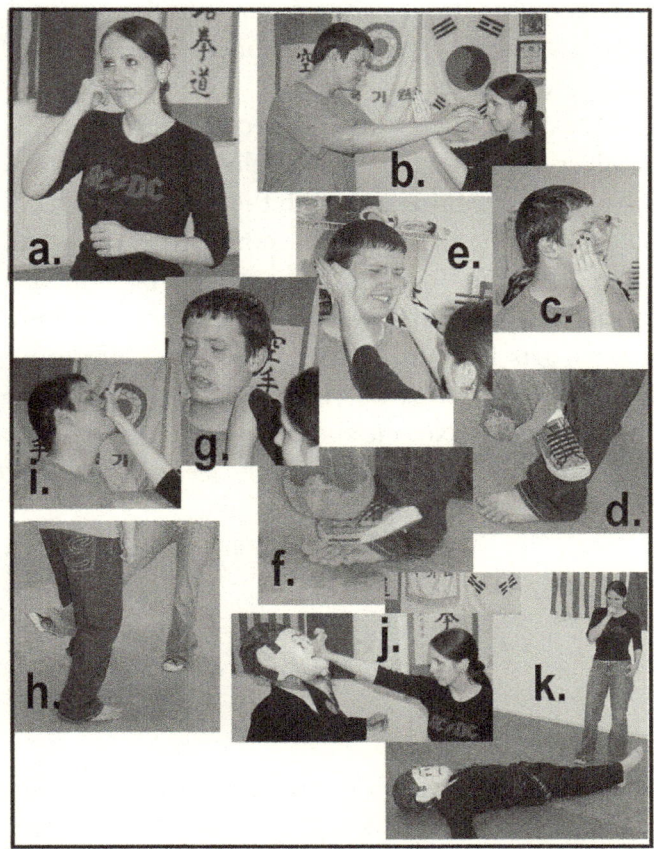

Figure 13: The Recipe

The figure above is intended for a final review of these important concepts. The concept of relaxing is given in a. above as the *earring fiddle*. It is a casual position not to let your antagonist know you are ready. In figure b. the initial strike is deflected away with preying hands. The next defensive move c. goes straight for the eyes followed by 3 or 4 kicks to the shin as in d. In the next picture the defender slaps or claws the ears as in e. followed by 3 or 4 stamps to the foot, as in f. Then the defender elbow strikes the attacker as in g. and delivers a hard kick to the groin h. The final defense is several rapid palm strikes to the nose, lips and chin, i. Photos have been used here to add emphasis to the ease and realness of the techniques. The models are Keely Dixon 1st Dan Black Belt and Keith Dixon 2nd Dan Black Belt.

This may appear to be more than is needed, but the sequence can be adjusted to deliver more or truncated to deliver less. The overall approach is to keep the opponent off balance with the high low high counters. The final two pictures in the figure are to remind you that nothing is better than practice. At a good martial arts school the student will get the opportunity to practice at full power with a real target. If it is not possible to go to a martial arts school the techniques here in this book will allow you to deal with most attacks. The only caution is that you must throw your self into the process. No one should live in fear. So lift up your head and remember you to can slay the Bear it is deep in your make-up.

Appendix A:

Other Bears That Come In

Sometimes nurturing requires Tough Love. The child with a sickness that causes him to thrash about and perhaps hurt himself must be restrained. Put this picture in your mind when dealing with self defense. The recalcitrant child that requires a smack on the behind for its own safety is a natural reaction for the nurturer. The strike to the attacker's nose that causes it to bleed is just an attitude correction. So, we turn back to the base idea of the village and the primal urge for self defense. The woman is defending against the bear not because of fear for herself but because of fear for the young and old people in the village. A man that strikes a woman can just as easily strike a child next. You as the nurturer must prevent that more than worry about yourself. Just as the soldiers worry about protecting the others in their unit the nurturer should always be thinking of protecting the helpless around her.

The best place when the bear comes into the village is out with the men. Or to put it another way, the best self defense is your not being there. But you cannot assure that this is always the case. If you depend upon your senses sometimes you can avoid problems. Like the women in the village you have a primal sense of survival about you. You have felt it.

It is the hair standing up on the back of your neck. If you go into some area and the smells, sounds, and environment tell you to leave then don't ignore them. This is your instinct kicking in. If you are in a conversation that is about to turn bad and you sense this feeling do not ignore it, leave and seek out another place or go to the earring fiddle position.

What this section of the book will do is to review other methods or scenarios of self defense not already covered by the basic set. Then you can go back and read the section again and understand the mechanisms of self defense. It is important at this time to get in front of you techniques to use so you can evaluate them and see how simple they really are and provide you with the feeling that this is accomplishable. They are grouped into the general type of attacks; front, rear, high, middle, and low. This is done so that later on when you come back to read this section again after you understand the process of self defense it is a simpler matter and not as daunting.

Attack to the Front High

A Face Punch

This is an attack from primarily a man to a man. When this attack is done to a woman it is intended to do severe facial damage to intimidate or punish. The strike can come: directly at the face as a snapping like punch, a lunging like punch, a circular punch, or as an upward punch. For the untrained individual it will come from the primary hand, the hand used for writing by the attacker. For the trained attacker it will come as a pair with a leading jab with the forward fist followed by a reverse punch as in the manner of a boxer. Again this does not come without signals, a motion, a look, a sound, an argument or some other signal. As previous in the book position the hands in what is called the yin yang position with one high and one low (earring fiddle position). The upper hand can casually fondle the earring while the lower hand fiddles with a button on the blouse.

Straight Punch

The straight punch comes straight at the face of the defender. As the attack comes the hands are used to pull the attacking hand(s) downward and pin them at a lower position. While one hand is pinning the hand is striking the face with a palm strike. There should be four to five palm strikes in a matter of three to four seconds. The defender moves during this period to a position almost to the side of the attacker. The defender then does an ax kick to sweep the leg of the attacker. This is done by kicking high with the leg next to the attacker and on the down stroke hit the back of the ankle or lower leg to kick a leg of the attacker out from under him. At the same time the defender does a forearm strike to the throat of the attacker. An alternate approach would be to do a side kick to the knee and a ridge hand to the throat. The defensive attacks are all done with multiple loud screams.

Lounging Punch

The lounging punch or haymaker is a punch generally thrown in anger and in an uncontrolled manner. It means committing the weight and momentum of the attacker into the punch. This commitment is the general source of his undoing. As with the large ship moving through the water it is hard to stop the forward motion but a little tug boat pushing on the side can redirect the very large ship in another direction.

The defense for such an attack is generally based on changing the momentum or removing the foundation of the attacker. The choice of the method depends on the difference in size between the attacker and the defender. If two people are about the same weight, then as the attack comes the defender ducks under the attack allowing strike to go over her body. When she feels the side of her body touch the lower body of the attacker she grabs the clothing of the legs or the legs and holding tight rotates the far shoulder downward as she stands up. When she stands up the attacker will rotate over her back landing on the ground. She can then seek escape.

If the defender is smaller than the attacker then by the nature of the way men are constructed and physics of motion, the defender can have faster hands. Before the attack comes the hands should be positioned as if offering something about mid-chest level. As the punch comes the hands should be placed with a leading hand on the outside of the attacking hand, wrist, or arm and the second hand as a picking hand against the hand, wrist or arm. The picking hand is used to pull in the direction of the strike or to push the strike to the side. As the hands come upward to the striking hand and arm the body rotates to get out of the way of the strike. Following the leading of the strike you can use the pin, strike, pin, strike routine to attack the face. Generally at this point you are to the side of the attacker and can now kick the knee. When he is on one knee a push kick to the back will drive him to the floor. You can then seek escape.

If the defender is of equal size or slightly smaller and the lunge has a good amount of speed the defender can catch the arm with yin yang hands. The yin yang hands catch the arm such that the forward part of the arm is captured by the downward stroke of the upper hand and the under part of the upper arm of the attacker is captured by the defender's lower hand moving upward. With a slight turn of the attacker's arm to the outside an arm bar is created. The defender then moves backward with the attacker's lunge while turning in the direction of the attacker pulling the arm with her to create additional momentum. The forward part of the attacker's arm is then brought downward and back in a circle about the point where the defender has a grip on the upper arm. As the attacker's hand passes the vertical position moving backward the attacker is thrown forward on his back. At this point the defender should be able to make an escape.

If the defender is of equal size with the attacker there is a simple take-down that can be done. As the punch comes the defender pushes the hand closed or to the center of the attacker. Quickly the defender spins her back 180 degrees and uses a spinning hammer to shock the attacker by either striking the face or kidney area. Generally the face has more shock effect and the hand is in the right place for the next part of the technique. Immediately after the strike the defender slips forward placing the front leg behind the attacker to act as a fulcrum. The hand that has just done the hammer strike then rises over the attacker's head and does a ridge hand back into the attacker's throat for a takedown. This should allow for an escape by the defender.

Although much time was devoted to this attack it is not generally one of the important attacks in women's self defense, and is more often found in an angry male on male confrontation. The ego of most men that strike a woman would not feel threatened enough to do such an angry movement. For the case of the abused female in a relationship with the abusive male this strike is used when other means of intimidation have failed and the male is in a pattern of increasing violence The abused person should beware because the next step in escalation is life threatening.

Sucker Punch

The sucker punch is done by distracting the eyes of the defender with a jab to the face while the other hand comes around to hit the head from the side. To do this properly the attacker must have had some training. The name of the attack indicates the attacker in some way has fooled the defender. If you are in an abusive relationship with someone with martial arts or boxing training then run for the door. For the nurturer, you are faced with a predator without remorse. There is no changing him. There is reasoning with him. There is only suffering.

The defense is divided by those of equal weight and those of smaller weight. For the case of defender and attacker of equal weight, since the attack is circular the defense is generally from the inside. This is a dangerous place for the lighter weight individual and can subject you to a choking hold. To do the defense you can direct the combat toward a sweeping takedown or a throw, but both techniques require someone near to equal weight with the opponent.

The throw is managed by blocking the inside of the hooking punch, moving in quickly holding the upper arm for the punch, grabbing the attacker with the other arm at the waist, and placing the hip into the pelvis area with the knees bent deeply. By the defender bending her knees pulling the upper body of the attacker downward and over the pelvis and then straightening up the knees the attacker will rotate over the hip for the throw. At this point seek escape.

For the sweeping counter, the block is also on the inside of the hooking punch, followed by rapid palm strikes to the face. The leg of the defender is maneuvered behind the leg of the attacker as the palm strike sequence occurs. A forearm strike is then done to the throat of the opponent. At the same time the defender does a high ax kick sweeping through to take out the legs. At this point seek escape.

For the lighter weight defender you must rely on quickness. As with the Lunging Punch given above, before the attack comes, the hands should be positioned as if offering something about mid-chest level. As the punch comes the hands should be placed with a leading hand on the outside of the attacking hand, wrist, or arm and the second hand as a picking hand against the hand, wrist or arm. The picking hand is used to pull in the direction of the strike or to push the strike to the side. As the defender's hands come upward to the attacker's striking hand and arm the defender's body rotates to get out of the way of the strike. Using the attacker's own motion you can the pin the strike against his body and use strike routine to attack his face. This is the pin-strike-pin-strike routine. The pin-strike-pin-strike routine is to pin the striking hand of the attacker with one hand of the defender while striking with the other then switch hands and repeat as often as necessary. Generally at this point you are to the side of the attacker and can now kick the knee. When he is on one knee a push kicka to the back will drive him to the floor. You can then escape.

The important question is how do you know it is coming? The attacker will give you signals. These signals are a slight dip down and away of the forward shoulder, eyes moving horizontal, and the rear foot moving up on the toes. The movements are subtle and the defender must develop the senses to see them. The nurturer has these senses. The child comes in with that certain look on his face. You say what have you been up to? He makes that slight glance in the direction of the offense and you know.

The nurturer knows the look but may need practice on what it means. If you are worried about your virginity they say Get *thee to a Nunnery,* but if you are worried about your life, then, *Get thee to a martial arts studio.*

Choke from the Front Two Hands

The defender is choked with two hands. If the defender focuses only on the choke and freezes then all of the training in the world will do her no good. To prevent this, focus on the task at hand. Most of the routines for a single hand choke work with a double hand choke.

The defender can shock the attacker and then peel off the two choking hands by grabbing the thumbs and rotating them outward using a thumb crank. This will free the defender from the choke. The defender then does sufficient counters to escape. The problem here is the hands of the attacker. If the attacker has hands that are much stronger than the defender she will not be able to break the hold this way. The defender must decide before she chooses an escape method about the attacker's strength. If she chooses wrong then she has a big problem. This decision must be made and executed in a matter of seconds. There are several options available.

The defender can reach over one choking arm to grab the other hand at the chopping edge where the little finger begins. Using the pressure point in the hand between the thumb and first finger, the hand can be rotated toward the center of the attacker and peeled away. Once the hand is peeled away the defender can use sufficient counters to allow her to escape.

The defender can chop down on both elbows pulling them to the outside, or the defender can palm strike upward on both elbows shoving them outside. Either strike will free the defender from the choke. She can then follow-up by moving into the center of the attacker with counters to allow her to escape. The recommended counter uses the high low high low approach.

Knife Downward

The attacker comes at the defender with a knife raised above his head. The strike must be blocked or the defender must step out of the way. Generally stepping out of the way is not going to work because the attacker will pursue the defender. Blocking the downward stroke must include securing the stabbing hand. For the nurturer if you are going to drop into the deer in the head lights mode, then you are not protecting your family, because you are soon dead or injured.

One option is to do a high block with one arm while bringing the other arm up under the attacker's elbow and back around to grab the wrist of the attacker. This will create an elbow crank. If the defender places one foot behind the attacker on the side of the stabbing arm he can be easily taken down. This routine however has some problems. If the attacker is significantly taller than the defender the technique will not work because of the length of the forearm. Further in performing the block, the defenders arm almost always is cut.

Another option is for the defender to grab the stabbing arm just below the wrist with both hands. This will stop the jab and generally does not result in a cut for the defender. As the defender moves forward toward the attacker the movement will create an elbow crank. To secure the elbow the defender can lower one hand to grab the elbow. By moving forward and doing an ax kick the defender can take down the attacker.

The floor work in both cases is the same. The knife must be controlled. As the attacker goes down the defender rolls him on top of the other arm, places a knee on top of the arm with the knife and then extracting it.

Attacks to the Middle

Hand Shake Grab

The hand shake grab is used to pull the opponent in range of the opponent. If the defender attempts to pull back it is a contest of strength. Using the principle of non-resistance, the counter is for the defender to step forward with the foot of the shaking hand across the opponent turning 180 degrees. In most cases this will free the defender from the grip.

If the attacker and defender are of equal weight then the defender can add the following technique to the turn. The defender reaches backward halfway through the 180 degree turn to grasp the attacker's arm with the hand that is not involved in the shaking. As the turn is completed, a pull by the defender will cause the attacker to go down to the ground. This happens because the attacker's arm is in an elbow crank due to the turn.

In either case as the defender becomes free she must follow up with multiple strikes until she is sure the attacker is sufficiently distracted to complete the escape without him chasing after her.

Grab to wrist two hands

In this case the attacker has occupied both of his hands in securing you, leaving his lower body open for kicking. The shock part of this defense routine is to kick the shins, stomp on the instep of his feet, and kick the groin. There are several methods for escaping the grip; two simple techniques are listed below.

The defender grabs his right hand with his left hand. This triangular set up with the shoulders makes a strong configuration. By moving both hands in a large circle the defender's grip is loosened enough to escape.

The defender opens both arms wide. As the attacker senses this movement there is a tendency by the attacker to force the defender's arms back in position. When the defender senses this change in direction he rapidly brings his arms together. At the center point the palm of one of the defender's hands will strike the wrist of one arm of the attacker knocking it loose from the grab. At this point the routines for a single grab can be followed to secure an escape.

At this point the defender does enough counters so an escape can be made from the situation and area.

Kick

An attacker that is attacking a woman does not often kick with any sophistication. This is caused by a severe underestimation of the woman as an opponent. The kick of choice is then a thrust kick toward the stomach. This kick is subject to grabbing as it reaches the apex, where it momentarily stops before it goes backward. If the defender moves backward a small amount she is out of the power range of the foot. The foot then comes up short and can easily be grabbed and raised or twisted. This motion will take the attacker down and provide time for the defender to escape. Of course a kick in the groin after the attacker hits the ground would provide some added time to escape, but be careful in kicking a downed opponent because your own feet are subject to being grabbed.

Knife Upward to Front

The attacker coming at you with a knife in an upward arc has held the knife in a stealth position and has clear intent to kill and to kill in a manner that provides a slow death. For the defender this is a very dangerous situation and first she must stop the thrust. But more than just dealing with the attack she must be prepared to deal with the intent. As with most attacks there are several ways to counter the move, but which ever is chosen the knife must be secured.

The most natural method is to block the thrust with an open hand X block. If the right hand of the attacker is coming forward then the defenders right hand should be on top in forming the X block. When the thrust is stopped fold the top hand downward to capture the hand by grasping the chopping edge of the attacker's hand. In the process of stopping the thrust the defender steps back with one foot to a wider more stable stance. The foot that goes back is the right foot if the attack is coming with the right hand of the attacker. After the hand is secure rotate the hand using the chopping edge toward the center of the attacker. At the same time rotate the second hand in the X block to the outside of the attacker's center. The hand will rotate naturally into the place between the thumb and first finger. When this is done the arm is in an arm bar and the attacker is rotated slightly sideways. Quickly kick the leg behind the knee with a side kick to take the attacker down on one knee. The arm of the attacker must be maintained in an arm bar with the elbow locked at all times. Using the arm bar the attacker can be pulled face down to the ground. At this point bend the arm to a point behind the back of the attacker so the knife can be extracted. Unless you know you have help available do not attempt to secure the attacker. Take the knife and escape, discarding the knife as you do so in a place where it is not easily retrieved.

Another approach is a crescent kick defense to knock the knife away or the arm to the side. In this defense the defender must run in and pin the knife arm to the chest of the attacker and then do a hook sweep take down. This approach generally is less attractive to the nurturer because of the need to rush in close to the attacker.

Knife Swiping

In a knife attack where the attacker is swiping his knife back and forth he is clearly trying to keep the defender at bay which indicates fear. There are two vulnerable points where the knife can be secured. They are at the ends of the swipe. At each of these points the knife stops and goes in another direction. The defender must rush into the danger zone at the apex and grasp the hand. If the attacker has more strength, then this is a dangerous approach. If you are faced with doing the task the take-down must be rapid. The position after the rush must be as follows: the defender must be side by side with the attacker facing in opposite directions. One hand must have hold of the wrist with the knife while the other hand strikes the throat in a Tiger Mouth strike or a Cobra Strike. Once this position is assumed the defender does a hard Ax Kick Sweep take down. As the attacker goes down, the defender drops to a position with her knee on the arm of the attacker to secure the knife. The attacker will attempt to rise. With the hand that struck the throat repeatedly strike the eyes, face and throat of the attacker. When the attacker is distracted remove the knife and escape.

Bear Hugs

A bear hug comes in two forms 1) where the arms are pinned to the body and 2) where the arms are above the hug. If the arms are not pinned then the attacker's face is open for strikes and many of the previous routines fit well. If the arms are pinned then the response is more limited.

If the size of the defender and attacker are such that the feet of the defender are on the floor then the defender can begin kicking the shins, stamping on the feet, and kneeing the groin. The defender can also strike the attacker's nose and lips with her forehead. This can cause a bloody nose which will distract the attacker. When the hug is slightly loosened then the defender can open the arms wide to shove the hugging arms of the attacker over her head. Once the defender is free then the defender can follow the routines of shocking, attacking the legs and when possible escape.

If the size of the defender and attacker are such that the feet are above the ground then she should use the *Sack of Potatoes Method*. A 50 lb sack of potatoes or deer corn is hard to pick up because it is dead weight and has the tendency to slip out of your hands. This is an application of non-resistance. Just go limp. As with a sack of potatoes, the attacker will have to loosen the hug to get another hug that is closer to the center of gravity of the defender's body. At this point the defender then opens her arms wide to free herself from the attacker and begins the shocking procedures.

The primary discussion here was for bear hugs from the front but bear hugs from the rear have much the same procedures.

Attack to the Side

Clothing Grab Side High

A grab to the clothing from the side can be done much as the *Come Here Babe* routine above. With grabbing the clothing there is another alternative in that the fingers tend to get trapped in the clothing. For a situation where the defender and attacker are of equal height the defender can quickly assume a position along the line of the grabbing arm by stepping backward. At the same time she can rotate her arm over the attacker's grabbing arm and back around locking the elbow straight in an arm bar. This is followed by a ridge hand to the throat or a claw to the eyes of the defender. Since you are side by side with the attacker he may try to hit you with the free arm, but by backing up and maintaining the side by side position this can be avoided. To take down the attacker do a side kick into the knee with the leg that is near the attacker. Once he is down on one knee then walk forward until he is completely down on the ground. This should provide enough time for an escape.

Do not worry about modesty, it is often overrated. If the grabbing of the clothing pulls open a blouse do not look down, do not let it occupy your mind and do not stop to deal with it. Modesty is a luxury. Worry about it in the police office filling out the reports on the attack.

Attack to the Rear High

Clothing Grab Rear High

The likely place for a grab to the clothing from the rear is the collar of the shirt or a belt or garment at the waist. If the attacker grabs the blouse, skirt or other garment by just grasping the cloth you can generally pull free with just a jerk. The thing that the attacker has done at this point is to occupy a hand in a place where his own hand can become entangled. Here the defender needs to use her senses. She needs to know in a flash which arm the attacker is using to perform the grab. The senses can tell you this bit of information if you just remain calm. The defender turns to face the attacker by rotating toward the arm that is grabbing. This rotation will place the defender's body against the back of the arm causing an arm bar, with the attacker's free arm as far away as possible. The rotation of the defender's body will provide enough momentum to overcome the strength of a much larger attacker. If the defender rotates in the other direction it will place her in a position to be encompassed by the attacker's free arm so the defender must be sure of the direction of rotation. By extending her arms the defender can use a hammer fist or claw to the face of the attacker as a shocking mechanism. Securing the attacker's arm from getting free the defender immediately side kicks the leg at the knee. At this point the defender frees the attacker's arm and kicks the back to complete the take down. This should provide time to escape.

In a grab to clothing that can be easily pulled free the defender's job is more difficult. The defender must turn and face the attacker and be ready for the next move by the attacker. The best position to assume is a stance with the feet not together and not far apart with the hands in a high low position. The defender should assess the surroundings without looking and watch the triangle formed by the head and shoulders. The slightest movement of this triangle will indicate the direction of the attacker's next move.

Hand Choke from Rear

The choke can be one hand or two hands. With one hand the defender can slip away by turning her body toward the thumb of the attacker. The defender then turns to face the attacker.

For a two hand choke, the attacker was able to put himself in such a position. After it is all over and the defender is sitting down with a cup of tea thinking about it she should say, *Shame on me for letting him get in that position.* With a double hand choke the attacker's weak points are the elbows and thumbs. The attacker's feet are just behind the defender's feet and open for a foot stomp. The attacker's body is in a position just behind the defender's body and open for elbow strikes. If the choke is not tight, then shock by stamping the feet before beginning the defensive moves. If the choke tight the defender must go directly to the defensive moves. The defense begins by throwing all of your weight at 45 degrees backward toward one of the attacker's thumbs. The pressure is then against one of the attacker's thumbs. At the same time the defender elbow strikes upward toward the elbow of the arm of the attacker's other arm. The elbow must be rotated outward and upward. At this point one of attacker's thumbs has pressure backward and the other has a twisting moment on it. If done properly this will relieve the choke and provide a path for escape for the defender and she is facing the attacker. The defender must immediately go into the shocking defensive response until able to escape the area.

Arm Choke from Rear

These chokes come in several forms: the Half Nelson, the Full Nelson and the Choker Hold. This is another place where the defender needs to chastise herself for letting herself get in this position. This position does not happen all at once. The attacker must come up from behind and put an arm around the neck of the defender. First, try not to get into this position by turning to face your opponent when you see the beginnings of the technique.

In the case where you were not quick enough, you are faced with a couple of possibilities: an arm around the throat and the other arm 1) holding the mouth, 2) holding one of your arms, 3) holding your shoulder or other part of your body or clothing, or 4) pressing on the side of your head to maintain the choke hold. The last case is particularly bad because this is the sleeper hold and you only have a matter of seconds before you pass out!

At the first signs of this attack if you cannot roll away and out of the attack tuck your chin. By doing this your throat is protected from the choke by your chin. This will temporarily thwart the attack but you must quickly take steps to deal with the attack. Begin elbow striking rapidly. Bite the hand if it is at your mouth. Bend forward at the waist to see the feet and begin stamping on the instep. Reach across your body and upward to the thumb of the hand of the choking arm. Grab the thumb and pull outward creating a thumb crank. Step outward and turn in the direction of the choking arm and deliver a knee or kick to the groin. Then begin the up down rapid striking and kicking procedure until you can escape.

Another technique to use is a quick throw if you are approximately of equal weight and a little shorter. After the tucking of the chin to protect yourself, grab the choking arm with both hands. Jump to a wide horse stance and bend forward at the waist to a point where the head is approximately level with the knees. If this is done rapidly the attacker's center of gravity will pass over the top of the defender's center and he is thrown forward on his back. This technique however is not generally one favored by women without some training.

The final approach is to use the sack of potatoes approach. After the tucking of the chin make your body completely limp and just sag downward. The attacker in order to maintain the hold must rely on you to stand up. Generally the choking arm will slide upward along the face. When the choking arm is to the top of the head, shove it upward and turn to face your opponent. Then begin the up down rapid striking and kicking procedure until you can escape.

Hair Grab Rear

The hair grab from the rear is much like the hair grab from the front. Here is another place the defender must sense which hand is grasping the hair. This is the side to which the defender must rotate. If the attacker grabs with the right hand the defender reaches backward with her right hand and visa versa with the opposite hands. With the correct hand the defender, reaches backward to hold the attacker's grabbing hand securely to the head pressing it as hard as possible downward with the and upward with the head. This will relieve the pain of the pull immediately and fixes the hand of the attacker in place. The defender then rotates in the direction of the grabbing arm creating an arm bar. The free hand of the attacker is rotated away from the defender. By bending at the waist the defender will cause the attacker to bend at the waist. A side kick to the knee will generally take the attacker down on one knee as well as free the defender from the hair grab providing the defender an opportunity to escape.

Half Nelson

The Half Nelson is a hold by the attacker where the attacker is behind the defender. The attacker places his arm between the defender's arm, upward and with his hand behind the defender's neck. The attacker's other arm is used to secure the defender from moving. Again, with many of these complex attack scenarios the attacker limits his own actions. The general rule for non-resistance says that if the attacker wants you then you give him what he wants in abundance. This will put him in a position of having to deal with the inadequacies of his own attack. To do this the defender backs up toward the attacker causing 1) the defender's feet to reach the attacker's, and 2) the attacker's locking elbow bent in a vertical position. The defender shocks the attacker by stamping on the attacker's foot. The defender then squeezes the locking arm next to her body to loosen the attacker's grip behind the neck. When the attacker's arm is vertical it becomes an elbow crank with the fulcrum as the defender's forearm. The defender then places the leg below the attacker's locking arm and behind the attacker's leg that is directly under the locking arm. Using the elbow crank the defender pushes outward with her other hand on the wrist of the attacker's locking arm. By turning slightly toward the attacker the defender pulls back on her tripping leg and the attacker will go down on his back. This should give enough time to escape.

Low Attacks All Sides

Tackle

This attack is not generally done by a large male on a smaller female because it requires him to dip too low. However it may be done by a smaller male on a large female. First the defender must stop the charge of the attacker while positioning her legs such that they are not together and one leg is back to form a good stable stance. To stop the charge do a double open hand push on the shoulders of the attacker while slipping backward maintaining the same stance. The follow up strikes to shock the opponent depend on what target is available. Remember, the attacker is after your legs so keep them away. Slap or claw the ears, gouge the eyes, elbow the shoulders, push him downward, and knee the face. If he raises his body upward keep the counters going without let up. The object is to get the attacker distracted or the attacker's eyes tearing so an escape can be made. Do not kick; he is in a position to grab your feet. His advantage is crouching and his stance is strong, however it is also his disadvantage. He cannot move fast. The defender can move faster. The attacker can be pulled off of his feet by pulling him forward. His clothing can be pulled over his head. His head can be twisted to bring him down. Using his head as a lever his body can be twisted. There are several routes to success.

Foot Grab

The foot grab can come in a number of situations. If the defender is in the process of doing a self defense technique and kicks high enough grabbing, then the defender is in trouble. The foot can be easily twisted to throw the defender to the ground. If this happens then the defender must use ground work to defend her so review the section on that subject …

Another foot grab is the one that gets played up in newspapers. Where there are two attackers and one is under the car, the feet of the defender are grabbed as she unlocks the car. There are several things wrong with this scenario. Most cars are too low for this to happen. The vehicle must be something like an SUV to have enough space for a full grown man to get under the vehicle. Next, the man under the vehicle is in a very restricted space and has limited options for an attack, which means there is another attacker to come up to the defender while she is dealing with the foot grab.

The defender probably sensed the danger in the situation as she approached the vehicle and failed to read it. The feet and legs are stronger than the hands. Kick backward or jerk the foot upward while supporting yourself with the car. Then the defender must turn to face the second assailant. Assume a position with yin yang hands and if possible move to a position where the two assailants are in a line and keep them in this position. The samurai Musashi called this *stringing fish on a line*. The first attacker in line must be disabled quickly. Swinging a heavy purse, briefcase or computer to strike the head is good. A kick to the groin is good. Quickly closing the distance to attack the eyes is good, or all of these counters and more. The situation the defender wants to create is for the second attacker to have to step over or walk around the first attacker. This will cause fear, momentary timidity in the attackers giving time for the defender to seek escape. The position to avoid is getting sandwiched between two attackers.

Ground Work

Face to the Side Attacker Behind

The attacker is trying to hold the defender but most of the defender's body is free to move. The defender rapidly elbow strikes backward with the upper arm while shoving the lower arm outward. This movement will rotate the upper body toward the attacker. The defender raises the knee of the upper leg and kicks backward at the legs of the attacker while twisting the hips toward the attacker. Once the face of the attacker is within range then the defender gouges the eyes, slaps the ears, claws the face and palm strikes the nose and throat in rapid succession. When able the defender knees the groin. The defender continues this counter until the attacker is so distracted that the defender can escape.

Face to the Side Attacker on Top

In this case the defender is on her side on the ground or a on bed with the attacker on top of the defender pressing down. The escape technique is one commonly used in wrestling. The defender makes a motion with her legs as if running. The friction of her body on the ground surface will cause her to spin about the shoulders or the place that is held down by the attacker. The grip of the attacker is loosened during this process and the defender will end facing the attacker. The attacker's arms and hands are occupied trying to hold the defender, so the attacker's face is undefended. The defender counters with strikes to the face, eyes, ears and throat. If possible escape immediately otherwise the defender is faced with using one of the other techniques until escape can be made.

Face Up Attacker on Top

Somehow the defender is down on the ground or the floor with the attacker on top. There are a couple of possibilities 1) both or one hand is pinned by the attacker's hands, or 2) both hands are pinned by the legs of the attacker. In both cases the counter generally begins with the defender shoving her pelvis upward several times causing the attacker to move forward and up the body of the defender giving the defender room to raise her knees so the feet are flat on the ground.

In the case where the hands are pinned above or near the head by the attacker the defender has a couple of options for a counter. The defender can feint surrender long enough to get something in range to bite. Another option is to kick one leg upward and hook the heel around the attacker's head and neck to pull him backward and off.

In the case where both arms are pinned with the legs, the defender shoves the hips upward enough to allow the arms brought together. Lock the fingers of the two hands together. Using the feet, legs, and hips shove upward with the lower body. At the same time the locked forearms shove the attacker's body forward. This will allow the defender to slip out under the legs of the attacker and be able to turn and face him. The attacker is required to turn around giving the defender a slight time advantage to prepare for rapid counters to the face to allow her to escape.

Face Down Attacker on Top

Here the defender is prone on a bed or on the ground with the attacker on top of her. The attacker can have the defender's arms pinned with his hands or trapped in his legs. The attacker is interested in holding the defender down. The defender's thrust is to try to rotate her body so she can use her arms, hands and legs against the attacker. The defender uses her knees, elbows and hips to bounce up and down to allow her to twist around. Once the defender is turned around to face the attacker the techniques given for a defender face up can be used.

Face Up Attacker Standing

The attacker will try to come in the defender's direction. The defender spins around so the feet are between her and the attacker. When the attacker is in range she kicks in a bicycle-like fashion toward the knees and shins. The defender must be wary of having a foot grabbed. As the attacker moves to get at the defender from a different direction the defender spins to keep the feet between her and the defender.

When the attacker comes in quickly and gets to a point a thigh length away, the defender spins around quickly reaching behind and grabbing both legs of the attacker with her arms. The defender then leans backward and raises her hips off the ground in a rapid thrust. The attacker's feet will act as a fulcrum and the attacker's legs as a lever to drop the attacker to the ground backward. At this point the defender rises to her feet and makes an escape.

Appendix B:

What the Village Shaman Should Have Told You

Given here are some sensible precautions that you need to think about as you go about your life. They are a compilation of many things you have heard before, probably from your mother. However you cannot live in fear. To go about your life from day to day you may have to do some things listed here as questionable but do not be fool hardy and be extra cautious in these cases. There are many books that discuss this subject[1, 3, 4, 5]. What I have attempted here is to take some of these concepts along with information imparted to me as an instructor by individuals seeking self defense training to develop an improved list in a format comfortable for the nurturer. As with all things it is important to always continue to improve the product, therefore you as an individual may have additional ways to improve your safety beyond what is listed here.

Dating

Know who you are dating: address, phone, occupation, habits, personality, goals, hobbies, age. Talk to others that know your date. Know where you are going and how long the date will last. Tell someone else of where you are going and how long it is to take. Inform your date that someone else knows where you are going and will expect a call from you when you get back.

Parties

Do not consume alcohol or drugs and avoid parties where there is excessive drinking or the use of drugs. Do not let others handle your drinks. If there is a lot activity, drink only from a freshly opened bottle. If some environment does not feel right, don't go there. Trust your instincts. Wear appropriate clothing. Do not participate in wet tee shirt contests, flashing, mooning, or otherwise expose yourself.

Home or Apartment

When moving in check the security of the area so you know you have a secure place. Change the locks and check the security of entrances into the residence, locks on doors, windows and sliding glass doors. Make entry a multiple step process, install peep holes and chain locks.

Now that you have a secure place to live use sensible rules when answering the door. Do not open your door to a stranger unless you are sure of the purpose of his visit and request identification of any person indicating they are a policeman or repairman. Don't accept just a business card as his identification card. Do not allow small children to answer the door. If someone asks to use your phone for an emergency, dial the number for him without allowing him into your home or apartment. Never admit to anyone that you are home alone.

Maintain a secure exterior image. List your residence in the phone book and on the mailbox using only your first initials. If you have obscene phone calls, don't say anything. Report the call to the phone company and/or police department install caller ID. If the call happens a second time, then report the number to the phone company. If you leave your home leave a light on inside the house, or the television set on, and turn on your outside porch light. Never leave a note on your door since this tells a burglar that no one is at home. Keep drapes, blinds, or shutters closed when you are disrobing. If you return home and suspect that someone has broken in, do not enter. It is possible that the burglar is still inside and you will place yourself in a dangerous situation. Know your neighbors and try to form community-neighbor watch groups for mutual benefit and safety.

On the Street

Now you have left your secure home and are on the street. If possible avoid walking alone, avoid walking down unlighted streets, and avoid taking shortcuts through parks, alleys, parking lots or questionable neighborhoods.

There are things you can bring on your walk: a flashlight, whistle or handy alarm device. Keep pepper spray or tear gas on a key chain in your hand when walking in strange neighborhoods at night.

If you believe you are followed by another person, stay calm and continue walking, cross the street, change your pace, and seek a place of safety. If it is not possible to do this then, allow your follower to pass you by. If he stops, you should turn and face him since you stand a better chance in a face-to-face confrontation than with your back turned. If you are followed, do not return home since you are vulnerable when opening the door and this will give your follower your address.

If you are followed by a car, walk up a one way street, change direction, and take down the license number of the car. If the car stops alongside of you and someone tries to force you into the vehicle, scream loudly, and try to run to the nearest place of safety.

Be aware of places an attacker might hide: between buildings, near garbage cans, under stairways and parking lots. Do not walk too close to bushes, trees or entrances to alleys and buildings. Walk facing traffic so you can see cars approaching you. Do not walk when you are emotionally upset, drunk or depressed or on medication. Do not go window shopping alone at night.

Car and Driving

Keeping yourself safe when you are driving is again based on using some common sense. Check your back seat before entering the car. Have your car key in your hand when you leave the office or home to go to your car. Keep doors locked and windows rolled up. Avoid side streets and try to stay on highways or major traffic areas. Keep your car in good operating condition. Always make sure you have enough gas for your trip before you start. Do not pick up hitchhikers. Do not leave your purse on the seat with the door unlocked. Sound your horn if someone tries to force entry into your car. If your car has mechanical trouble on the highway, pull the car off the road, put your scarf on the or handkerchief on the external mirror and lift the hood and lock up in your car. Ask someone to call for help.

If you are followed by another car, drive to the nearest police station or public area with many people and take down the license number of the other car. If someone tries to force you off the road, do not pull over to avoid damage to your car. Maintain control, continue driving, and get a complete description of the other vehicle. When filling your car with gas do not return to sit in the front seat and then return to the gas nozzle directly without touching metal to avoid a static electric charge ignition of the gas fumes.

Riding with Someone Else

Do not hitchhike. It is dangerous. Never ride with a driver who appears unsafe to you. Never ride with someone who is or has been drinking. Always ask where the driver is going, before telling where you are going.

Sit next to the door and know how the seat belts, door handle and door locks work.

Public Transportation

If you use a public bus or transportation at night, wait in busy, well lit areas. Plan to travel in groups if possible. If you are on an almost empty bus, sit near the operator. As you get off the bus, check who gets off with you. If someone suspicious seems to be following you, head quickly for the nearest store or busy area. If necessary, call police or friends for help. Always keep your purse close to your body when shopping or when you are on public buses or transportation.

Appendix C:

Teaching Self Defense

This section deals with teaching Self defense. It is important to understand how self defense is taught to improve your learning of it. The second reason for this section is to tell the reader how good self defense is taught so that it will encourage the reader to search out a local instructor for hands on instruction. The practice of self defense under a good instructor is good for the mind, good for the body and good for the spirit.

Teaching by the Numbers

Many schools teach self defense routines by the number. In other words, when your attacker does a punch to the face do techniques 12, 18, 21, 23 or 43. The other approach is to use cutesy little names to use as memory hooks such as do the bear claw, dragon's breath or something like that. Both of these methods rely on the student memorizing many routines.

Teaching by Reaction

The alternative is to teach by reaction to a particular attack. For a particular attack the instructor goes through the Five Principles of Self

Defense one at a time. This is done for many attacks and many potential first approaches at non-resistance. Then for each attack sequence many approaches at summoning your Ki are practiced and so on. The process here is to simulate the decision tree formed as both the attacker and defender vary their reactions. The process is to use slow motion and slow counters to develop a complete self defense routine. The routines are repeated many times at increasing speed. When the speed of the routine is high then a difference is entered into the routine on either the attacker of defender side. This process is varied until four or five complete routines are developed.

The next practice involves doing these routines in slow motion perhaps to music in a manner similar to Tai Chi. The music is part of developing an external focus. Take downs are only done to a point of breaking balance so that the set of routines can continue uninterrupted. After this is mastered then the routines are done in a rapid manner without the attacker knowing what is coming next.

The goal of practice in this manner is to develop Mushin, the ability to do the routine with out thinking of the process or thinking of a mental listing of various techniques finding the best fit for the present situation. This teaching approach uses the recipe for self defense. To compare it to cooking it is something like turn on the oven, mix the ingredients, pour in a pan, bake until done and serve. But, as with any recipe you do not want to leave out a key ingredient. It is a shifting recipe that must be put together. The goal is to get to the point where when you are finished with the recipe you do not worry whether you have added the pinch of salt. In oriental teaching, a routine is repeated over and over until it becomes a blindly natural thing to do. In western teaching philosophy, the teacher asks questions until the student realizes that they knew a thing all along. If you combine the two teaching approaches repeating a routine several times asking questions of the student about understanding the grand philosophical and scientific concepts behind why the technique works. The result is hopefully a realization by the student that they understood the application of the philosophical and scientific principles all along and now they can use them as tools for many situations, not just the particular one that was originally practiced.

Classroom Routines and Procedures

Exercise and Student Preparation

To avoid common muscle pulls and other injuries it is necessary to warm-up the students before any training is done. Most schools have a set of exercises they follow. It is important to stretch every time you train. Do not skip these routines in favor of learning more in a given class.

Learning How to Fall

Falling is particularly hard for women because it is not a natural process for them. Your mother always told you be careful and not to fall down. Women then in turn do that with their children. When they fall and there are tears they hug the child and sooth hurt feelings. Therefore it would be nice to know how to fall without hurting yourself. Now I doubt a mother will look at a tearful child and say, *next time tuck and roll when you fall.*

Falling is a general part of the curriculum of martial arts. Students learning self defense must in particular practice falling on a regular basis as part of their training. Working in pairs one student will often be thrown to the floor during the routine. The falling can produce injuries unless safe falling is practiced. There are also routines that require falling in order to perform the routine (sacrifice routines). As a general practice, falling is taught from the final position (fallen) to the initial position (standing). This approach allows the student to know what is coming when he/she falls. Once the falls are taught to the class they can be quickly done as part of the general warm up. Depending on the size of the studio and the size of the class it may be necessary to do some of the falls one at a time by the students. Each of the falls should be practiced at least twice on a regular basis to make them part of the automatic response of the student when they are needed. Given below is a description teaching each of the major falling routines.

Hip Break Fall: Start the falling process by having the students lie on the floor and roll up into the position just before the fall. This is the ending position for the fall. The following steps construct the fall backwards.

1. Lay the students on their back. The students raise both of their legs in the air and roll to a sitting position. Repeat this process several times

2. As the students roll forward one leg is tucked under the other. For each roll forward have them switch the tucked and extended legs. Repeat this process several times.

3. Continue the forward movement in the forward roll until the student is on one knee with the tucked leg behind at 90o to the foot on the floor. Repeat this process several times alternating the tucked leg.

4. Continue the forward movement by having the students rise to a standing position. Repeat this process several times.

5. The final part of the routine is to perform the routine backward by tucking the leg sinking to the hip and rolling onto the back and shoulder. At this point students of the same sex are able to push each other over to practice the falls.

Arm Break Fall—Right & Left: There are three basic falls of this type: roll to the right and left and straight back. These are taught from a deep squatting position as the initial step. They should be done both to the right and left.

The fall is taught in the following manner.

1. The students extend the matching leg and arm on one side of their body (right/left). At this point, because of balance the student will roll onto his/her side. Have the students slap or hit the floor with the extended arm. Repeat this process several times.

2. The students now start from a standing position and slowly squat to the previous starting position and follow the routine of number1 above.

3. The students speed up the process gradually until they are comfortable with the falling process. At this point students of the same sex are able to push each other over to practice the falls.

Arm Break Fall—Straight Back: This fall requires the student to fall on to the back using another part of the body to absorb the shock of the fall. It is not an easy mental process because it is easy to get hurt. The student must learn to land gently. In a philosophic sense he/she must become one with the floor. The fall is taught in the following manner:

1. The student squats and extends both arms. As the student rolls onto the hips and back, both arms are slapped against the floor. Repeat the movement several times.

2. The student squats and extends both arms. As the student rolls on to the hips and back, both upper arms are struck the floor. The entire surface of the back of the arm is used to absorb the shock of the fall not the elbow itself. Repeat the movement several times.

3. Gradually have the student start from a standing position, squat and then do the fall. As the student becomes comfortable the process can be sped up until the student can do the fall from the standing position.

Knee Break Fall: Falling forward requires a certain amount of courage on the part of the student, because the floor is coming right at their face. This fall is a fall from a squatting position. The knees and the forearm break the fall. However, falling on a hard surface can cause injury to the knees unless it is done correctly. The knees act as the fulcrum in the falling and the forearms act as the shock absorber in the fall. The primary direction of the fall is a rotation about the axis where the knees touch the ground.

The routine for learning is as follows:

1. Squat, extend arms and go up on the toes of the foot. The action of going up on the toes starts the rotation forward.

2. Fall forward to the knees.

3. Break with forearms—The forearms are bent and must strike the floor a split second after the knees strike. The entire forearm must strike

the floor at the same time. In particular students have a tendency to put their hands out to stop the fall. This is where wrist injuries occur. The force should not be along the arm but at a direction nearly perpendicular to the wrist joint.

Arm/Side Break-Fall Right and Left: The Arm/Side Break-Fall can be done backward to ease the difficulty of fear of falling. The routine is for the students to lie on their shoulder with the (right/left) arm extended. The leg of the extended arm (right/left) is also extended. The opposite foot (left/right) is placed behind the leg (right/left) on the ground at about the knee with the sole of foot on the floor. The students are then asked to roll up (to the left/right) to a kneeling position. After several times of raising to a kneeling position then do the falling from a kneeling position. The final step is to stand. From a standing position, first kneel then fall. After several attempts at his then stand and do the following complete fall.

1. Stand extend arm (right/left)

2. Extend same leg (right/left) across the centerline of the body to the (left/right)

3. Break-fall with arm and shoulder

Tuck Break Fall Right and Left: This fall is the same as the Arm/Side Break-Fall above except that the fall is a roll in the forward direction and the break-fall is with the arm, shoulder and upper back. It can also be taught in a piecewise backward manner.

1. The first step is to have the students kneel down on one knee (right/left). The other leg (left/right) is in front with the foot on the floor. The calf of the (right/left) leg is at about 130 degrees to the (left/right) foot on the floor.

2. The second step is to circle arm (right/left) until the top of the hand can be placed on the floor between the (left/right) foot and the (right/left) knee. The student leans forward until the forearm is on the floor.

The student then rolls onto the top of the arm and shoulder to the (right/left). After repeating this process several times the student then stands and can practice the fall from this position.

Classroom Etiquette

Etiquette is a very important part of establishing and managing a safe, disciplined, and learning environment when teaching one-step-sparring routines. For example, the seeming ritual of the attacking student stepping back into an attack stance with a scream allows a beginning that is always the same. The defending student beginning in a position with the arms down each time allows the same muscular reaction to occur. Muscle memory is very important for when the individual has to actually use the technique there will not be time to think and he/she will have to rely totally on the natural movement created by the muscle memory.

Signals

When a grappling technique is performed the attacker may use a Joint Lock or Throw or other technique that could potentially bring pain to the defender. The method for the defender to signal that he/she is in pain is to slap his/her side or leg two times with the free hand. At this signal the attacker must immediately release the defender to avoid injury.

Behavior

Students must always bow to each other before and after a set of one on one routine. After a routine that ends with one of the students on the floor, the standing student must offer to help the grounded student to his/her feet. Students must always work in the same sex pairs, never in opposite sex pairs. If the number in the class is odd, then the odd student works with the instructor.

Appearance

Because of the close proximity of students in the routines students must come to class in a clean uniform, without body odor or bad breath. During the course of the class students will sweat and during grappling techniques students should be prepared to deal with an opponent that is sweaty. Students must always return their uniform to a neat condition after each technique. Students must try to avoid tearing their partner's uniform.

Safety

Safety in the classroom must include the total environment and the total activity in the classroom for every second for effectiveness. There are several key areas to review: creating the correct environment, conducting class in a correct manner, avoiding common injuries, and maintaining awareness of activity in the school.

Environment

The school must have the usual open spaces provided for TaeKwonDo instruction free of obstructions that can be hit by the students while doing the routines. For the self defense routines in this guide, the school should be equipped with the following additional equipment: throwing mats, personal safety equipment such as groin pads, eye shields, and helmets.

Standing Routines

Line routines are to develop fast and natural reactions with the hands. In line routines are for practicing techniques against an imaginary attack. By its very nature it is impossible to do routines where the student must adhere alone. Such routines require a second student. Line routines can be practiced for the basic hand and foot work for both escapes and captures '; however again, the techniques themselves can only be practiced with another student(s). The line routines are done to develop rapid hand movements that become instinctual in nature. They are done routinely at almost every class as a warm-up. See the chapter on hand movements.

One Step Routines "Formals"

The use of walking routines is primarily for practicing self defense routines using either right or left hands and feet. They can be done in lines by the entire class. The routines can be repeated many times to develop muscle memory. The general method is to do the walking routines several times and then follow them with a two person "formal" routine with two people facing others.

Formals are done as follows. Two people face each other at an equal to two arms lengths. They begin with a bow. Then the attacker steps back in a long front stance, low block, and screams. The attacker then steps forward and punches with either a right or left hand at face level. The defender then performs one of a series of pre-staged routines against the particular attack. These routines are sometimes referred to as one-step sparring.

Multiple Step Routines

The use of walking routines is primarily for practicing self defense routines using either right or left hands and feet. They can be done in lines by the entire class. The routines can be repeated many times to develop muscle memory. The general method is to do the walking routines several times and then follow them with a two person "formal" routine with two people facing others.

Appendix D:

Terminology

The teaching of Martial Arts has a vernacular that is particular to that activity. This section gives definitions and descriptions of unusual terminology that appears in the book.

Adherence: Adherence is the practice of the hands, arms and body of the defender by adhering to the attacker without actually grabbing or capturing the attacker. This technique often uses open hand blocks to redirect the opponent's attack. In self defense the act of the block to redirect the attack is carried a step further by allowing the blocking hand or foot to stick to the opponent long enough to place the defender into an advantageous position. The *wives tail* for the master's test for adherence is the inability of a fly to take off from the master's hand because every time the fly bends its knees to jump off the skin the master raises his hand so the fly is unable to take off. Realistically, when the attacker's hand is blocked and moves away, the defender's blocking hand moves with it to maintain the ability to redirect its motion

Arm Bar: The defender reaches across her body to the grabbing hand. The finger tips will feel the hardness of the back of the hand then the softer feeling chopping edge of the hand. The thumb is placed finger tip pressing in at the soft spot between the first finger and thumb. The second hand comes up under the attacker's wrist in a picking hand approach to grab the wrist. Using both hands the defender rotates the attacker's hand toward the thumb. The hand of the attacker is pushed toward the attacker's shoulder as the arm is twisted causing the arm to lock at the elbow. The thumb of the defender is pressing on the back of the hand of the attacker and the attacker's fingers are pointed upward. With the arm locked at the elbow it can be used as a lever to manipulate the body of the attacker positioning him for further counters.

Ax Kick Sweep: In the ax kick the leg raises high and then chops downward striking with the heel of the foot. The kick is particularly useful in self defense to strike the back of the heel, ankle or foot to kick the feet out from under an attacker. If the two individuals are side by side facing in opposite directions a slight push on the upper body as the ax kick is done will take down the largest opponent.

Ball of Hand Strike: The ball of the hand strike is made by opening the fingers wide from the thumb. The strike is made by shoving the open hand between the thumb and the first finger into the target in a manner such as to strike with the ball of the first finger. The hand can be closed to grab the target area after the strike. This is another strike used mostly on the throat. For the nurturer this strike is not a killing strike but will cause the attacker to choke momentarily. This is escape time for the defender.

Captures: Captures are the process of grabbing an opponent to do a self defense technique. The attacker is primarily striking at the defender. The capture grabs the striking component and often depends on the timing necessary to complete the grab at a speed superior to that of the attack. Speed is the ultimate determination if the capture will work and requires a lot of practice to achieve the necessary timing.

Charlie Horse: A Charlie Horse is pain caused by cramped muscles. You can cause a Charlie Horse by striking at 90 degrees to a muscle that is taut and squeezing it against the bone underneath. The reflection of the strike back added to the initial strike will cause the muscle fibers to cross and seize and momentarily give a numbness in the leg or arm that is struck. The strike must be severe and at the exact spot. Generally, this strike requires an extended period of training.

Choker Hold: The Choker Hold is a hold that when applied cuts off blood supply to the head by pressing against the main artery in the neck. This hold is done by encapsulating the neck with the arm and forearm from the rear and using your other hand to press the encapsulating arm further closed. The person in such a hold will pass out in less than 10 seconds. In order to apply such a hold one must be behind the choked individual in a superior position, (arm pit level with the neck of the choked individual).

Chop: The chopping strike is made by closing the finger and striking with the ridge of the hand at the little finger. To use this technique to injure a full grown man requires training and practice. This technique is not recommended for the untrained individual of slighter weight than the attacker. But if you are striking with everything you have in a shocking approach this is a good strike. The strike can also be used to bend or open a joint, block or cause a distraction.

Claw: Fingers can be used as a claw. The defender needs to have good fingernails and not the fake kind. If you are worried about ruining your fingernails you are thinking about the wrong thing. The claw is often used at the end of a palm strike. In this case the forward strike with the palm heel of the hand is punctuated by a clawing hand as you draw back.

Crescent Kick: The crescent kick is a kicking block. The crescent kick is a useful kick in that it can be used to kick a weapon from the hand of an attacker. The crescent kick is done by sweeping the leg in a circular fashion with the toes pointed up. The striking surface is the palm of the foot or the outside ridge of the foot.

Earring Fiddle: One hand is raised level with the face while the other hand is level with the middle of the chest or upper abdomen. The palms of both hands are facing each other. This is sometimes called the Yin-Yang position. The movement of the hands should be casual and apparently fiddling with the earring, eye brow, hair, buttons on the blouse or belt buckle. The position is a defensive position without seeming prepared to fight. The upper hand is in the shape of a hand about to pick fruit, *a picking hand.* The other hand is positioned at mid-chest with the palm turned slightly downward. The position is that of a hand used to pet the top of someone's head, *a petting hand.* The upper hand can be used to deflect the strike to the side while the lower hand can be used to deflect a lower strike to the side.

Elbow Crank: An elbow crank is created by bending the arm at the elbow then while holding the elbow in place pushing the hand or wrist across the normal bend of the arm while pulling the elbow in the opposite direction. The torsional force provided on the shoulder is significant.

Elbow Strikes: Elbow strikes are done backwards with the elbow and are good for distracting the attacker that is behind. If the positioning is such that the strike can be delivered to the head it can do some damage but not a lot of damage.

Escapes: An escape is the process of the defender extracting himself/herself from an attacker that has grabbed him/her. This process often depends on the dynamics of the individual grab. The dynamics of the grab can depend on direction of movement, what is grabbed, and the operation and pressure points of the hand, arm, and body.

Fingers: The fingers can be used to strike the eyes, throat or other soft spots. The strike used by the Three Stooges with two fingers can be used to strike both eyes but this strike is not as sure as using a spear hand strike to strike one eye. The effect will cause the eyes to tear and the attacker temporarily blinded in either case. The latter strike is easier to do in that you can hit one eye from many angles but both eyes require a strike from head on.

First Strike Position: The first strike position is where the attacker is within an arms reach without taking a step. To assume this position you need to back away without appearing to back away. To do this turn sideways in spot rotating on the foot below the arm that is fiddling with your earring. Count to five and then rotate on the other foot to a position facing the antagonist. Count to five and repeat the process. This will keep the upper arm in a leading position.

Flat Fist or Cobra Fist:: Fist strikes can be delivered in several methods striking with different parts of the hand. These strikes are always designed for specific targets to maximize the efficiency of the striking. If the first and second knuckles of the hand are bent then you create a flat fist. This fist has several names in martial arts, for example a cobra fist because its shape represents a cobra's head when it is flattened out. This fist is good for striking the throat, eyes or in some cases the groin or a tight muscle to create a Charlie Horse. For the nurturer a cobra strike will not kill someone but may cause that individual to choke temporarily. This is escape time and the reason to support doing it. You, as a nurturer, are needed by your family and that is more important than the well being of the attacker.

Forearm Strike: The forearm strike is delivered with the forearm and is useful in striking the side of the face or head. For example, the defender could kick the back of the knees with a side kick to take the attacker down to his knees. The defender could then step up hold the head in place with one hand and deliver a forearm strike to the ear of the attacker. The result would be a painful ear and the time to make your escape.

Hammer Fist: The hammer fist is made by closing the hand into a fist and then swung and swinging the bottom of the fist toward a target. The hammer becomes powerful if it is used in conjunction with a spinning body. The hammer is good to hit the groin when the attacker is behind the defender. The hammer is good to hit the side of the face or nose. There are other fist configurations that can be used and if the reader goes to a good martial arts school she will practice the strikes given above and learn others that are useful.

Hand Wrist Crank: A hand wrist crank is made by bending the hand and twisting across the axis of the lower arm. The leverage is the length of the hand to the center of the wrist. The attacker will try to pull away to relieve the hold but by pressing forward the control method can be maintained.

Horse Stance: This is standing as if you are standing in the stirrups of a saddle. English saddle riders become very strong in the legs standing in this stance. The horse stance is fundamental in martial arts. It is extremely strong from the side but not so from the front or back. The horse stance lowers the center of gravity and is often used in throws and other areas where upper body work is important. If you train in martial arts you will spend hours in this stance.

Palm Strike: The palm heel strike is the primary strike for women's self defense. It is used by striking the nose, philtrum of the mouth and lips with base or bottom of the open palm in an upward motion. To deliver the maximum power of the strike place one foot back and strike with the full body pushing off with the rear leg. The clawing hand is often used at the end of this strike by pulling downward with the fingernails. The strike may cause bleeding of the nose and lip and the eyes will tear. For the nurturer the strike is not a killing strike except in the movies.

Preying Hands: Preying hands are made by placing the palms together as preying in front of the upper body. Both hands are used by shoving straight forward and upward to spread the attackers hands and arms as they come foreword opening up his middle section for counter attacks.

Push Kick: The Push Kick or ball of the foot kick is done by shoving the ball of the foot straight forward at the attacker. The target is primarily the stomach. For the nurturer the most that can happen to the attacker is to have the breath knocked out. We have all had that happen and we survived. This should not be a problem for the nurturer to use this technique.

Nelson: A Half or Full Nelson is a grappling hold done from the back using one or both of the defenders arm pits as a fulcrum point for a lever at the back of the head.. The Nelson is completed by encircling the defender's arm with the palm of the hand(s) pressing on the back of the defender's neck. There are simple methods to get rid of these holds, but they are best learned in a good martial arts school. In general these methods involve using the force applied by the attacker against himself. By squeezing the arm off center the fulcrum effect is removed and by rotating to face the attacker the defender can easily get out of the hold.

Round House Kick: The round house kick requires some training to do properly and is generally not recommended for the untrained person to do in self defense. This kick is done by spinning on one foot and kicking to the side with the top of the other foot in a circular fashion. The striking surface is the top of the foot or the ball of the foot. If the defender has a little training this kick can be useful in kicking the knee to the side to assist in a take down.

Shin Kick: The shin kick can miss if you do the kick with the toes straight to the shin. Further it requires you positioned specifically with respect to the shin. A better way to kick the shin is with the side of the foot. Usually inside but the outside may be used as well. To add to the power of the kick hold the edge of the foot to the shin after the initial strike and slide it downward toward the foot using your sole edge of the shoe to scrape the shin. With a little practice you can make the foot go in a circular manner and deliver repeated rapid shin kicks that scrape along the shin.

Side Kick: The side kick and stomp kick are done the same way. The side kick essentially stomps to the side above the ground. The target for the side kick generally is the side or back of the knee. In certain positions there are other safe targets to strike with the side kick but the kick can be slow to do in comparison with other kicks and there is a probability of grabbing. The knee is struck to make it bend to take the attacker down so for the nurturer this strike will do little damage to the attacker but will help positioning him for the defender to escape. If the attacker's leg is locked and the kick is done directly into the front of the locked leg more damage can be done to the knee. If the nurturer again realizes that her family needs her to nurture them, then she can use this technique at will. Further there is some joy when she is in court and asked to identify her attacker she can say, *the one with the limp.*

Slap Ears: This defense is done by cupping the palms and slapping the ears. The cupped hands will cause an over pressure in the ear drum channel resulting in a ringing of the ears and temporary pain in the ears. The strike should be followed up with a pull back with clawing fingernails to create pain in the exterior ear.

Stance in Strategy as Given by Musashi. [8, 9] *Adopt a stance with the head erect, neither hanging down, nor looking up, nor twisted. Your forehead and the space between your eyes should not be wrinkled. Do not roll your eyes nor allow them to blink, but slightly narrow them. With your features composed, keep the line of your nose straight with a feeling of slightly flaring your nostrils. Hold the line of the rear of the neck straight: instill vigor into your hairline, and in the same way from the shoulders down through your entire body. Lower both shoulders and, without the buttocks jutting out, put strength into your legs from the knees to the tips of your toes. Brace your abdomen so that you do not bend at the hips.*

Stomp Kick: If you pick up your foot and stomp it on the floor the power comes from the thigh not the calf of the leg. These muscles are long and thick and can deliver a lot of power. The nurturer should not be troubled using this kick, in that in its most powerful form it is not life threatening unless it delivered to the throat which is an unlikely position for the attacker and defender. The target for the stomp is the foot of the attacker. The most likely use is to strike the foot. The heel of the defender's foot strikes downward on the instep of the attacker's foot. The result will cause the weight of the attacker to shift to the other leg and a weakness in the knee of the leg stomped upon. For the nurturer an attacker with shoes on the attacker at most will get a bruise.

Striking the Eyes: A woman, as a nurturer, will not naturally want to strike the attacker's eyes. She must be prepared to cross a mental boundary to use this strike. Your mother told you when you were young *not to run around with that pencil because you were going to trip and poke out your eye.* The eye moves in its socket when you press on it. It is just not that easy to damage the eye to the point where it is not useable. So if your life is in danger *Get Over It.* The nurturer does not want to hurt anyone or anything. There are ways to strike the eye without delivering permanent damage. Straighten the hand and strike with the tips of the three middle fingers just below the eye into the cheek bone. When this is done, the skin of the cheek will slide upward and be between the striking finger tips and the eyes. The strike will cause the eye to tear but the eye will not be permanently damaged. Other strikes that can be used in a similar manner are a cobra fist or an extended thumb.

Striking the Groin. This defensive routine is not done with a push kick. The striking surface is small in this kick and the defender might miss. The better approach is to strike with the entire shin having the foot stick out behind the attacker. The leg is raised upward in a stiff fashion with the knee locked or almost locked. If the kick is not accurate it will bounce off the legs of the attacker and still hit the target. For the nurturer, remember, you get over a groin kick but if the attacker knocks you in the head you may not get over it. Make your choice. The knee is often shown striking the groin in movies and TV, but this strike has limitations. If the attacker is much taller than the defender she will not be able to reach the groin with the knee. Further, in making the knee strike the defender is placed in a dangerous position by getting close enough to the attacker to make the strike.

Thumb Fold: The thumb is done by grasping across the attacker's thumb with the entire defender's hand and defender squeezing the attacker's thumb past the limit of its natural motion. The attacker's thumb is into the defender's palm heel of the hand while the attacker's hand above the thumb is held firmly by the fingers of the defender's hand.

Bibliography

1. D. Kim,. and J. N. Lee *Hosinsul Conceptual Self Defense*, Seoul KO, Nanam Publishing Co, 1979, out of print.

2. D. Kim, *Complete One Step Fighting*, Seoul, KO, Nanam Publishing Co, 1979.

3. Irwin Carmichael, *Women's Awareness Response*, Charlotte NC, Mati Publishing 1995.

4. B. Konzak, M. Konzak, S. Konzak, *Girl Power: Self Defense for Teens*, Canada Sports Books Publisher, 1999

5. Wiseman John, *The SAS Self Defense Handbook*, Guilford CT, Lyons Press, 1997.

6. R. Gracie, C. Gracie., *Self Defense Techniques*, Canada, Invisible Cities Press, 2002.

7. Yamamoto Tsunetomo, *Hagakure*, New York, NY, Kodansha International, 1979.

8. Musashi, Miyamoto, *a Book of Five Rings, Translated by Victor Harris*, Woodstock NY. Overlook Press, 1982.

9. Musashi, Miyamoto, *A Book of Five Rings, Translated by Stephen Kaufman*, Boston MA, Tuttle Publishing, 2004.

10. James Calavell, *The Art of War*, New York, NY. Dell Publishing, 1988.

978-0-595-47879-8
0-595-47879-4

Made in the USA
Coppell, TX
28 January 2023

11878838R00090